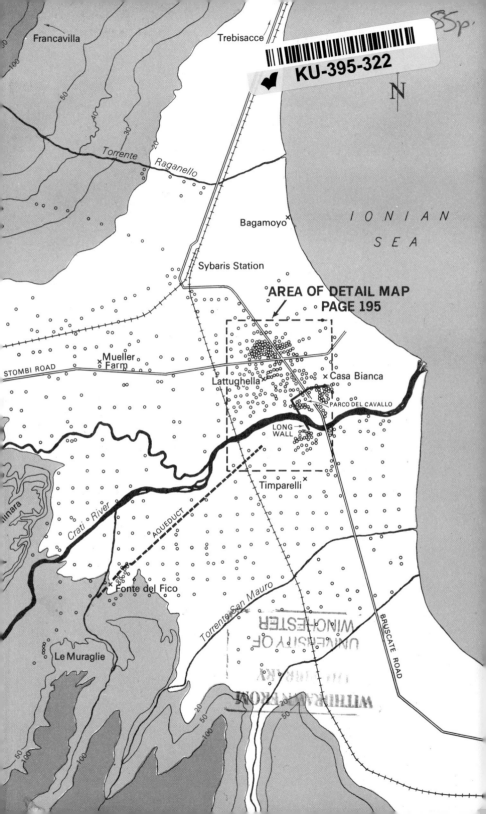

Francavilla

Trebisacce

N

Torrente Raganello

Bagamoyo ×

I O N I A N

S E A

Sybaris Station

**AREA OF DETAIL MAP
PAGE 195**

Mueller
× Farm

STOMBI ROAD

Lattughella

× Casa Bianca

PARCO DEL CAVALLO

LONG →
WALL

Timparelli

Crati River

AQUEDUCT

× Fonte del Fico

Torrente San Mauro

BRUSCATE ROAD

Le Muraglie

# SEARCH FOR
# SYBARIS

# SEARCH FOR
# SYBARIS

❦

## ORVILLE H. BULLITT

J. M. Dent & Sons Limited
London

Printed in Great Britain by
John Dickens & Co. Ltd, Northampton
for J. M. Dent & Sons Ltd
Aldine House Bedford Street London
First published in the United States of America

ISBN: 0 460 03979 2

Quotations from the following authors have been made from the translations of the Loeb Classical Library through the courtesy of the Harvard University Press: Appian, Aristophanes, Athenaeus, Cicero, Diodorus Siculus, Dionysius of Halicarnassus, Herodotus, Hesiod, Livy, Pausanias, Polybius, Procopius, Sophocles, Strabo, Thucydides, and Virgil.

Map on page 195 is adapted from a map supplied by the University Museum of the University of Pennsylvania.

# PREFACE

Sybaris, Greek history, archaeology, and writing this book have provided me with ten of the most interesting years of a long life. It did not occur to me to write about our work until a publisher, not the present one, suggested it. I was helped in many ways, although the writing is all my own. I want to thank those who worked over it with me, and the first is Barbara Rex, author and editor. It was she who went over the manuscript, page by page, with such comments as "You change tenses," "This is dull," but every so often "This is good." I make frequent references to Dr. Froelich G. Rainey and Elizabeth K. Ralph in the text, and they need no acknowledgment here. The work at the site was enormously simplified by the help and the knowledge of Signor Enrico Mueller and Signora Mueller. Their ability to obtain the cooperation of the local landowners was of inestimable value, and I shall always be grateful for their courtesy to me. George Stevens, my editor, has educated me in the pursuit of authorship with unfailing kindness, patience and humor.

Dr. Kenneth M. Setton and Dr. Rudolf Hirsch, Director and Associate Director of the Library of the University of Pennsylvania, aided me frequently in my study of the ancient authors. Dr. Lloyd W. Daly was never too busy to give me Greek translations and help with references. He was kind enough to read, for accuracy, my accounts of the ancient Greeks. Dr. Ellen M. Kohler provided knowledge of the dating of sherds and the accuracy of references.

Mrs. Maurice E. Green typed hundreds of quotations of the Greek and Latin authors, and Miss Cecelia C. Bavolek typed and retyped the manuscript. How either of them deciphered my writing is a mystery to me. David J. Crownover and Vittoria Vitelli, in Dr. Rainey's office, were more than helpful on many occasions.

Finally, my wife not only corrected and improved my English, but listened and talked about Sybaris to an extent that should have, but did not, strain over fifty years of marriage. At times she would look at me and say, "I see it coming over you; what is it this time?"

To all these kind people, I extend my deepest and most humble thanks.

ORVILLE H. BULLITT

# CONTENTS

# ILLUSTRATIONS

## PHOTOGRAPHS

## MAPS AND CHARTS

# INTRODUCTION

As a political negotiator during and after the last great war, there was a time when I concluded that myth and history are indistinguishable. If "consensus of opinion" writes history, then myths, which have the authority of faith, must be a part of what we accept as the facts of history. Still much of the excitement in archaeology surely lies in the discovery of hard, solid evidence that an episode in recorded history is real, in the sense that one can see and feel some tangible remains in the earth which relate to that episode. Many times during the past century we diggers have turned up that evidence—there really were a Troy and a Mycenae; the pool of Gibeon really did exist and you can see it today, dry and partially filled with stones, but a solid fact; Imhotep became a legend to the ancient Egyptians themselves, but inscriptions describing him and his architectural achievements are now as real as the Empire State Building. Things are solid facts. But the significance of those things probably will always remain partially embedded in myth.

Those many of us who have carried on the search for Sybaris probably will never explain to our own satisfaction just why the search has had such a fascination. From a professional point of view, my primary interest has been the development, during the search, of effective electronic instruments for archaeology, and also the demonstration that such instruments are capable of a new kind of archaeological survey. But, like Orville Bullitt, I was caught up in the search for its own sake. It was important to detect the actual site, its form and present situation, and to discover the remaining reality of a city which has become a legend, a moral lesson, a symbol, and a useful word in the English language. Also, we were picking up where others had left off, and there was a particular challenge to solve the puzzle which had engaged others for nearly a century. Why should the most famous of all the Greek colonies in Italy remain undiscovered? Was it actually the rich and luxurious place described by ancient writers, or had the myth developed over the centuries since it disappeared?

We know now that Sybaris, like Pompeii, had the misfortune to be located where, if the current theory of drifting continents is correct, two of the great plates of the earth's thin surface collide to cause earthquakes and volcanoes. In such a zone of conflicting forces, the land surface can shift at any moment and one tremor can mean the death of a city. Today the charred remains of Sybaris lie below a vast blanket of sterile clay sealed in the earth beneath a fertile plain. No wonder it has remained a mystery—no protruding columns, no mounds, no scattered fragments of pottery on the surface to give a clue. Its existence and its destruction are hard facts. Its significance in the ancient Greek world probably will always remain a matter for conjecture based upon fragments of the written records and whatever may be turned up eventually in probes beneath the burden of earth.

For me the high point in the search was not that day in 1965 when we finally saw for the first time the actual foundations of buildings in ancient Sybaris. We were much too busy then with pumps, generators, a collapsing caisson, and workmen who did not wish to risk their necks in a deep cut which could trap them at any moment. It was, rather, a moment during the same year when an amplifier boomed out with a sudden rising and falling pitch. Sheldon Breiner and Elizabeth Ralph had rigged up a new kind of sensing device, with equipment used in a satellite to monitor magnetic intensity in outer space, but jerry-rigged for land survey and wired in with soldering wire, pliers, and other tools to stabilize the current from an erratic generator. Jacinto carried the sensor across a field of sugar beets, and we waited in suspense until he passed over the point where we knew a stone wall lay deeply buried in the clay—then the sudden wail on the amplifier and we knew that the device would work and that it would be possible to design an instrument sensitive enough to detect the deeply buried ruins of the archaic city.

One can only imagine how much Pythagoras of Croton, the experimental scientist of Miletus, and their followers in Sybaris would have appreciated such an instrument based on the oscillations of electrons, and a rubidium atom. They were the ones who conceived of the atom, and we are the ones who now make use of the forces locked within those atoms.

This search for Sybaris, indeed, is more than a treasure hunt or an attempt to unravel myth and history. It is part of the current exciting process of applying science in the creation of tools to explore the nature of the world we live in.

Orville Bullitt began with a romantic interest in the discovery of the tomb of Alaric and ends up financing experiments in far-out electronics. But wherever this search has led him, his enthusiasm has never wavered. In fact, it was his determination which kept us going during periods when the solution of the enigma of Sybaris seemed quite impossible. His account of the search includes all the myth, legend, and history, as well as the facts as we all see them at this point. It is his book, and certainly we have no quarrel with it. Quite to the contrary, reading over this account of the Search, so skillfully blended with the ancient records of the city, the people, and the custom of that time, I am struck with the way he has put life and action into this kind of research. For all of us engaged in the Search it has been exciting and filled with suspense, but to convey our excitement to others is not easy. I think Orville Bullitt has done this and in doing so has performed a very real service to archaeology—a scholarly discipline which succeeds only if it has meaning for intellectually alert people in all walks of life.

FROELICH G. RAINEY
DIRECTOR,
MUSEUM OF THE UNIVERSITY
OF PENNSYLVANIA

# SEARCH FOR
# SYBARIS

# I

# SYBARIS
# 720-510 B.C.

"Quaff Chian from great Sparta stoups, gorge like a Sybarite, get very drunk, yet all the time keep pleasant and polite."

Thus did Aristophanes describe the men of Sybaris in his "Men of Dinnerville," Fragments of Attic Comedy. Today, twenty-five hundred years later, the words "sybarite" and "sybaritic" are still part of our language. Webster defines a Sybarite as "one of the inhabitants of ancient Sybaris, noted for their love of luxury and pleasure; hence [often not cap.], a voluptuary."

Although the city of Sybaris, built in the arch of the Italian boot, existed only for some two hundred years, from the eighth to the sixth century, its citizens grew enormously wealthy and lived a life of ease and luxury beyond that known to any other great Greek city. Many ancient writers, whose accounts we will come to later, describe their dissolute ways, leading to the final ruin of the city and its sinking into oblivion. Only the name remains.

1

The Plain of Sybaris

The search for the lost city combined so many exciting and challenging elements that for generations the intense interest of archaeologists has been aroused. The romantic history of Sybaris, sung by authors since the days of Herodotus, establishes it as probably larger and wealthier than Athens, containing treasures comparable to those in the homeland. The sudden and complete destruction of the city in 510 by Greek neighbors in the city of Croton was as complete as that of Pompeii. The ruins should disclose a unique example of a seventh-century city, buried for over two millennia. No other great city of the past, about which we know so much, remains unexcavated and provides the promise of such an extraordinary reward once its secrets are uncovered. In a moment of enthusiasm, an eminent archaeologist even prophesied that its discovery would be as momentous as the finding of Troy.

The problem was to find a city of perhaps two square miles in area in a plain of four hundred square miles. The city might lie twenty or more feet below the soil carried down from the mountains for twenty-five hundred years. Many have tried and failed, and it has been only since the development of electronics and other modern methods that the search could be carried out on a truly scientific basis.

The incentive for the search for Sybaris related here was, therefore, twofold: first, the possibility of unearthing untold treasures of the past while acquiring knowledge of the culture and life of seventh-century Greece; second, and equal in importance, the proving of the value of a totally new method of archaeology. With the instruments which were to be used, hitherto unknown in this field, it might be possible to locate and outline buildings lying well below the ground level and thus perhaps revolutionize future archaeological work. Success in either of these objectives would be a satisfying reward. Naturally, success was hoped for in both.

The start of the search for Sybaris was by the back door, and occurred in a rather roundabout way. During the winter of 1957 I had been reading Gibbon's *History of the Decline and Fall of the Roman Empire,* and I became deeply interested in his account of the Visigothic king, Alaric, who was born about A.D. 364 near the mouth of the Danube.

Alaric had always been somewhat confused in my mind with Attila the Hun, but the more I read about Alaric the better I liked and admired him.

Whereas Attila was a brutal barbarian, Alaric by comparison was what might have been called in later years a gallant knight. He had been well-educated as a Christian at the court of the Eastern emperor, Theodosius, in Constantinople, and his brother-in-law married Theodosius's famous daughter, Galla Placidia. Her magnificent tomb in Ravenna, with its blue-and-gold mosaic work, is one of the great works of art of the fifth century A.D. When Alaric conquered Rome in A.D. 410, he treated his foes, and the city itself, in a far different manner from that of those Christians, the Crusaders, who six centuries later were to massacre all the inhabitants of Jerusalem. Indeed, in our own time we had the edifying example of that hero of the British Empire, Lord Kitchener, when he captured Omdurman, first desecrating the tomb of the Mahdi, the leader of the Saracens, and then carrying off the Mahdi's head in a kerosene can as a trophy.

The full account in Gibbon of Alaric's capture of Rome held great appeal for me. His entry into Rome was made possible by disgruntled slaves, of whom there were forty thousand in the city. They opened the Salarian gate to his troops. Many fortified cities in the past were captured not by force, but by a traitor within who opened a gate to the enemy. Although pillaging took place, Alaric respected the churches and spared the lives of all those who did not resist. The slaves, however, took every opportunity to avenge themselves, and the streets were filled with dead bodies.

Alaric's army marched out the Appian Way, loaded with gold and silver from the palaces. His dream was to conquer Sicily and then North Africa, but when he embarked most of his ships were sunk in a storm and he returned to Cosenza in the south of Italy, about fifty miles from our later goal of Sybaris. It was here he died and was buried.

Alaric's tomb, which is said to contain some of the spoils of Rome, including the fabled candlesticks of King Solomon, has never been found, and the possibility of unearthing it excited my imagination. I knew nothing whatever about archaeology, its problems, trials, hardships, hopes, and disappointments; and perhaps that was a good thing, because I was anxious to step in where professionals did not tread. My only knowledge was that an Italian engineer, Signor Carlo M. Lerici, had been having great success in locating Etruscan tombs by means of an electrical apparatus. It seemed to me, in my innocence, that this same instrument could be used to find Alaric's tomb and that in a few weeks we would have some worthwhile results.

I grew up within a short distance of the University of Pennsylvania and from my earliest childhood knew many people who were connected with the Museum of the University. Even at that time it was famous the world over for its work in archaeology and for the many highly successful expeditions it had carried out in the Near East. In one form or another I became increasingly involved with the University, having been a Life Trustee for more years than should be counted. Realizing the outstanding position of the Museum and because of my intimate association with the University, I naturally turned to them.

In a moment of enthusiasm I wrote the Director of the Museum, Froelich G. Rainey, asking if he would be interested in searching for the tomb of Alaric. I did not know Dr. Rainey, and his first answer was discouraging. He wrote that he had no idea where Alaric was buried. Luckily I had this vital information in a book by Jordanes, who wrote the earliest account of the Goths in A.D. 551. "Alaric," Jordanes says, "was suddenly overtaken by an untimely death and departed from human cares. His people mourned for him with the utmost affection. Then turning from its course the river Busento near the city of Cosenza . . . they led a band of captives into the midst of its bed to dig out a place for his grave. In the depth of this pit they buried Alaric, together with many treasures, and then turned the waters back into their channel. And that none might ever know the place, they put to death all the diggers." Cosenza lies inland near the toe of the Italian boot.

Having spent my life with business organizations rather than museum expeditions, I too easily assumed that, if relatively small Etruscan graves could be found by Signor Lerici with his apparatus, it should be a simple matter to discover a huge tomb full of treasure. When I discussed this with Dr. Rainey, he promptly told me that it had taken the Museum two years to locate the tomb of Gordius, even though they knew the exact mound in which it lay. Perhaps it is a good thing to be an inexperienced amateur. My spirits were not entirely crushed by his reply, for I still felt that with the new instruments Alaric would present no problem. When I saw Dr. Rainey, I knew immediately that we could work together. Attractive and handsome in his middle fifties, he made me feel at ease the minute I entered his office. With his sense of humor and lightness of touch, he was far from my picture of a professor of anthropology and one of the world's leading archaeologists.

Fortunately, it did not take him long to agree to undertake the search and to make a trial of new scientific instruments in the field of archaeology. Little did he know how involved he would become over so many years. For my part I have not regretted it, as the past years have been exciting ones working with him, and he has more than fulfilled his part by pressing the work with great vigor. The Museum has as many as twenty projects going on all over the world under the direction of members of the staff and under his general supervision, but he has made our search for Sybaris his own and has spent many months at the site.

For almost two years, "Fro" Rainey and I talked about the expedition, exchanged letters, and laid plans to find the tomb of Alaric. During this time he worked with Signor Lerici on the Etruscan tombs and was much impressed with the resistance apparatus being used which measured the electric conductivity of the soil. Rainey believed that much better instruments could be built in this country, especially with the enormous strides we were making in electronics. He told me that the Littlemore Company of Oxford, England, had also developed an instrument in conjunction with the University of Oxford. They agreed to send a man to cooperate in the work being done by the Museum.

As the exciting project matured, it seemed that perhaps we were on the threshold of a totally new method of archaeology. Up to this time the archaeologist had only limited choices. After reading every ancient historical account he could find about a lost city or tomb, he then went over the configuration of the ground and looked at aerial photographs. He might dig and be within a few feet of a new Venus de Milo and yet never find it. But now by simply walking across

a field with an instrument, he should be able to say, "Dig at
this spot and you will find a temple."

In the spring of 1961, Dr. Rainey and Signor Lerici set
off to locate the tomb of Alaric, and possibly do some work
at nearby Sybaris. In a letter he wrote me speaking of his
trip, he added, "since I know that Lerici has already located
the lost city of Sybaris!" He based this statement on the fact
that Lerici, with his instruments, had located a wall. Later,
after excavations, this was found not to be of the period of
Sybaris, but at the time it provided an added inducement. The
whole of the southern coast of Italy is a mine of archaeological
treasures in the many cities which the Greeks built there at
the height of their expansion. Sybaris, fifty miles northeast of
the site of Alaric's tomb, was the most famous of all.

As I had also done considerable reading about the riches
of Sybaris, I pictured that Fro would first find all the treasures
of Alaric's tomb and then move on that summer to begin the
work of Sybaris. He would perhaps be able to locate the city
near Lerici's discovery, and we could proceed to excavate the
following summer. How little I knew.

My first disappointment and realization of the difficulties
of archaeology came with the reports from Cosenza. The
aerial surveys of the valley of the Busento River had shown
nothing of value. In Alaric's day the river where he was
buried wandered through the quiet countryside; a small village
lay on its bank. Now the stream runs between stone embankments on both sides of which is a modern city. Alaric might
be underneath any of a dozen or more modern buildings. The
course of the river as it ran fifteen hundred years ago could
not be found. I had written to Fro in June to say that if Alaric
proved impossible, I hoped he would try for buried Sybaris.
Fortunately, he concurred in this suggestion, telling me that
Lerici's men, using his electric apparatus, had found the stone

wall a few feet below ground level, and he went on to say, "This may be the city wall, a harbor wall, or the base of an old aqueduct . . . and is almost certain to lead us to the city." This wall, about fourteen feet high, has since been excavated and is still a puzzle. The base is of fourth-century B.C. Greek blocks of stone and the upper part of Roman construction.

The north side of the wall is of rough construction and the south side smooth. We now believe the wall might have been a retaining wall of a port, since it was much too narrow to be a city wall used as a fortification. The later instruments traced it and a continuation at a right angle for almost two miles, but it has not all been excavated. This changed Fro's thought that Sybaris had been found.

The quest for Alaric was one of the shortest archaeological expeditions ever made, but it was in the genesis of this search that the work at Sybaris began. During the last few years I have sometimes felt that cutting the Italian red tape required as much energy, and certainly as much skill, as the actual digging. In order to do any archaeological work in Italy, permission of the Department of Antiquities of the Ministry for Public Education is necessary. This has not always been easy to obtain, and under Italian law all archaeological objects which may be discovered are considered to be State property and may not be removed from the country. A reward not exceeding 50 per cent of the value of the objects found may be paid by the Government and divided between the discoverer and the landowner. This might raise some knotty questions if we were to find King Solomon's candlesticks or the arrows of Hercules or a Sybaris Venus—all priceless.

Regretfully we abandoned Alaric to lie, perhaps forever, in his tomb and turned all our attention and efforts to the fabled city of Sybaris.

Many had sought in vain this fabulous city, the dream of

archaeologists, and we will read later, in Chapter X, of some of the principal ones who had endeavored to find it. In every archaeologist there must be a deep-seated sense of his youth, going back to the childhood Easter egg and treasure hunt. Every morning he approaches the dig with the same sense of excitement. Hope is always there, and in his mind the next day or week is sure to uncover something of historical significance. It was this feeling that buoyed us up over a long time in the search for Sybaris.

# II

# DEVELOPMENT
# OF GREECE

To understand fully what led to the building of Sybaris by the Greeks in 720, on this unknown shore of the Ionian Sea in the south of Italy, a brief account of the beginning of Greek civilization is necessary. The homeland of Greece had become overpopulated, and living was increasingly difficult. In various ways invaders from the north had exerted a constant pressure on the population of the Greek mainland. In prehistoric times Greece was inhabited by the Pelasgians, who may have been the progenitors of the Ionians, and Herodotus[1]* says, "What language the Pelasgians spoke I cannot say for certain, but if I may conjecture from those Pelasgians who still exist . . . they spoke a barbarian language." (The Greeks used the word "barbarian" to indicate a foreign people and not in our sense of the term.)

When the Greek mainland had little or no civilization, the island of Crete, one hundred miles to the southeast, was

---

* Superior figures refer to the Reference Notes at the end of the text.

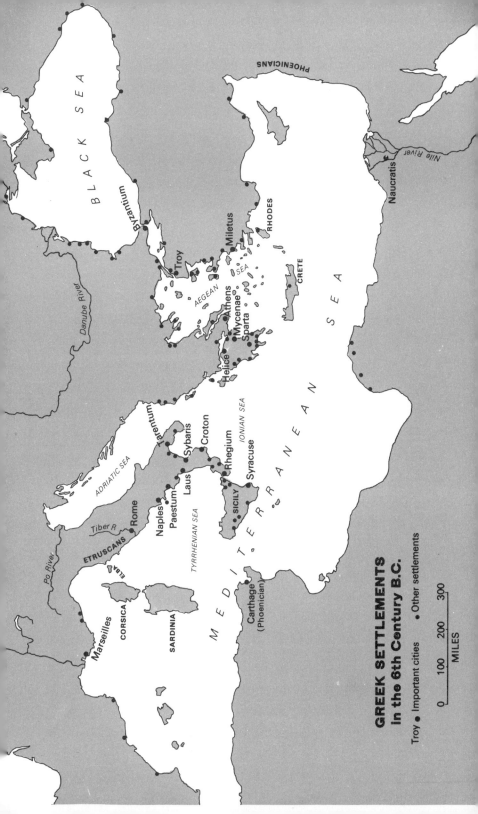

# GREEK SETTLEMENTS
## In the 6th Century B.C.

Troy ● Important cities   ● Other settlements

BLACK SEA

PHOENICIANS

Nile River

Naucratis

Byzantium

Danube River

RHODES

Troy

Miletus

AEGEAN SEA

Athens
Mycenae
Sparta

CRETE

Helice

MEDITERRANEAN SEA

IONIAN SEA

Tarentum

Sybaris
Croton

Rhegium
Syracuse

SICILY

Laus

Naples
Paestum

ADRIATIC SEA

Tiber R   Rome

ETRUSCANS

Po River

TYRRHENIAN SEA

Carthage
(Phoenician)

ELBA
CORSICA

SARDINIA

Marseilles

MILES

0   100   200   300

developing in the Bronze Age. About 1400 the great city of Knossos in Crete was destroyed, never to recover its eminent position.

Who these people of Crete were is still unsolved, and scholars differ as to their origin. However, they had developed the earliest written language in Europe, and they excelled in the arts of jewelry, painting, and pottery. In the Minoan Period they embellished their work with gold, and bronze was freely used. Iron did not come into general use until after their downfall. Thucydides has an account of King Minos as the earliest ruler who possessed a fleet. He controlled most of the Aegean Sea, and installed his sons as Governors of the Cyclades, and they cleared the sea of pirates.

The later Greeks believed in the legend of King Minos, who demanded from Athens an annual tribute of seven youths and seven maidens as an offering to the Minotaur. The story of Theseus and his entering the labyrinth to slay the Minotaur may well be connected with the great palace unearthed at Knossos. This palace had an elaborate and complex floor plan, and the design is attributed to Daedalus. Many feel that it is the actual building of the famous labyrinth, and it might easily have needed Theseus's plan of unwinding a ball of string behind him in order to find his way out. The palace, built over four thousand years ago, had the modern luxury of baths and drains, not to be equaled until our own times. The upper stories were reached by great staircases, with inner halls lighted by light wells.

The walls were covered with magnificent frescoes of members of the court and of athletes, both male and female, involved in graceful conflict with the Cretan bulls. Some athletes are portrayed grasping the horns of the charging animals and turning somersaults over their heads. These frescoes and also the impressions on clay tablets which have been found give a vivid picture of the life of the times. The Cretans even had a gaming board, similar to our chess board, made of gold, silver, and ivory.

As no great temples have ever been found at Knossos, there are many who believe that the King may also have acted as the high priest. In that case, this fabulous palace would also have served as the house for religious worship. No city walls have been unearthed, which may indicate that being islanders, and believing that they controlled the sea, the Cretans considered a wall unnecessary and were unprepared for the landing of the enemy who was to destroy them. The two great cities of Mycenae and Tiryns on the Greek mainland south of Athens, which were to succeed Crete in power, did not fall into this error, but were built with a citadel within a fortress. These cities first appeared in the second millennium and after Crete's downfall were powerful until the twelfth century.

As recently as January, 1966, the Greeks found a royal tomb on a hillside ten miles from Knossos which had been untouched by grave robbers, the bête noire of all archaeologists. Those who excavated it suggest, from the robes richly covered with gold sequins, the necklaces and gold objects in the tomb, that it may indicate a Cretan civilization going back to before the year 3000.

The story of the discovery of the great Aegean cities is a fascinating one which in a sense begins with the discovery of Troy by that extraordinary scholar and inaugurator of modern archaeology, Heinrich Schliemann. Born in 1822 in a small village in eastern Germany, the son of a minister, he began reading about Troy at the age of seven and determined then that he would some day search for this fabulous city. At the age of fourteen he went to work in a grocer's shop and ended his formal education. His health was bad, with a weak chest, and his appearance was unattractive, but he was burning with ambition. Deciding to seek a fortune in South America, he set sail at the age of nineteen, but his ship sank off the Dutch coast and he went to work in a banking house in Amsterdam. His spare time was spent in reading, and he became an amazing linguist. In one year he learned English and French and went on to master Dutch, Italian, and Spanish, claiming that he could learn a language in six weeks.

He now began the study of Greek and became absorbed in the beauty of the language. Reading Homer in the original, he became fascinated by the accounts of the Trojan War and felt sure he could find the lost city of Troy, based on these descriptions. Just one hundred years later we were to begin our search for Sybaris, using the ancient accounts as the base for our conjecture as to where the city lay.

He quickly acquired Russian and when he was twenty-two established a partnership with a Russian in an import-export firm. Settling in St. Petersburg, he amassed a fortune. In 1851 he was in California acting as a buyer of gold dust from the miners and adding daily to his wealth; after a year he returned to St. Petersburg as a merchant prince. After trips to Athens, China, and Japan, he settled in Paris and at the age of forty-four became a student at the Sorbonne. In 1868 he had become so imbued with Homer that he went to Greece and decided to look for relics of Odysseus on the island of Ithaca. Nothing important came of this, and in a few days he was off to Mycenae, where he again failed to do any excavating. He was later to find great treasure, both here and at neighboring Tiryns. Moving on to Constantinople, he felt sure, from his knowledge of Homer, that the hill of Hissarlik contained the ruins of Troy. Frank Calvert, an Englishman who owned part of this site, had already done some digging and believed he had found the site of Troy. Calvert agreed to allow Schliemann to work at Troy. Schliemann did not return to start his work for two years, and in April, 1870, he dug for the first time. The story of his success has been told many times and of how he then went on to Mycenae and Tiryns.

Meanwhile, this extraordinary man had decided to take a Greek bride as his second wife and asked a friend in Athens to obtain some photographs of Greek girls and to choose one. A beautiful seventeen-year-old bride was found for him and, as she had the additional advantage of a thorough knowledge of Homer, they were promptly married. They were devoted to each other for the rest of his life, and she was a tireless supporter in his work. His final archaeological triumph escaped him on account of his own difficult character. In 1889 he decided to buy the uncovered site of the city of Knossos on the island of Crete, for which he had been negotiating for six years. The story is told that, becoming annoyed because he found there were fewer olive trees on the site than were claimed by the owner, he refused to complete the purchase and thereby lost the opportunity to make one of his greatest discoveries.

It was only later that Sir Arthur Evans, the British archaeologist, undertook the work. In A.D. 1900 he excavated the palace of King Minos at Knossos and gave the name of Minoan to the culture that existed there in 2400.

Evans had discovered more than a thousand tablets covered with hieroglyphics which were apparently in two different scripts. Scholars named these scripts "Linear A" and "Linear B." For years they attempted to decipher these tablets without success, and it was not until 1953 that an English amateur, Michael Ventris, found a clue to one type of script, the Linear B. Ventris was an architect who served in the British R.A.F. during World War II. He was a navigator and cryptographer, and although the earlier Linear A has not been deciphered, and much of the Linear B is far from complete, Ventris maintained that Linear B represented a Greek dialect and thereby influenced the thinking of scholars who, up to that time, had debated whether the language of the script was Greek. Ventris's further work was cut short by his tragic death in an accident. The deciphering of the Linear B script makes it almost certain that the late Minoan civilization of Crete was essentially the same as that of Mycenae and that both were the forerunners of Greece itself.

Thucydides[2] tells us that before the Trojan War the mainland of ancient Greece was not settled with any fixed villages and that migrations were frequent, each tribe leaving its land when it was invaded by a more powerful foe. There was no trade, but each village tilled its own soil; the villagers planted no orchards and had no surplus wealth, for they had to be ready to flee the invader, especially as their towns had no walls. The best land, that of Thessaly and Boeotia, and most of the Peloponnesus, was first conquered and then settled by the invaders. Attica was comparatively free from these invasions because the soil was not rich, and it therefore continued to retain its early inhabitants. For this reason Athens grew and flourished; the leading men of other cities, on being driven from their homes, moved to Athens and became citizens in a firmly established community.

The Athenians claimed that they were descended from the original inhabitants of Attica and that Athens was the metropolis of the Ionians. In the thirteenth and twelfth centuries, when the great civilization of Mycenae in Greece was at its height, a series of invasions by tribes from the north took place. The first of these hordes are only vaguely known as "people of the sea." They were followed by the Dorians, a Greek-speaking tribe coming from the direction of Dalmatia and Albania. These warriors had a new and secret weapon which enabled them to defeat their opponents: iron. The bronze swords and shields of the native Greeks were no match for this new metal which the Dorians had used to forge their swords. By about 1100 they had wiped out the Mycenaean cities and had brought about a period of over three hundred years of darkness in Greece. Except for the sparse countryside around Athens and the city itself, the Dorians drove out the Ionians, who fled to the shores of Asia Minor and the numerous intervening islands. The Dorians pushed south and established their capital at Sparta, which they settled as a military encampment. The characteristics of these two peoples differed greatly. The Dorians resembled what we consider to be the typical Prussian: disciplined, warlike, brave, ruthless, and unconcerned throughout most of their history with the arts, literature, or philosophy. The Ionians, on the other hand, believed in the freedom of the individual both in his thought and his political life.

The Ionians bestowed the greatest honors on those who excelled in literature, philosophy, drama, music, and sculpture. What we have absorbed from the Greeks in our own culture must be attributed to the Ionians, who scorned the regimented, untutored, and Spartan life of the Dorians.

The Sybarites held the Dorians in low esteem; both Athenaeus[3] and Plutarch[4] tell us of the Sybarite who went to Sparta and was entertained at a public banquet. On his return he told his friends that it was no wonder the Spartans were the bravest men in the world, for anyone in his right mind would prefer to die ten thousand times rather than share such poor living.

I like to imagine the conversation of two Spartans on hearing of the death of Socrates. "I had word from Athens that Socrates took the hemlock." "I remember him; he was the hoplite who saved the life of Alcibiades at the battle of

Potidaea." It all depends on your point of view as to what is important in life. To the Spartans he was but a soldier, to the Athenians a great philosopher.

Prior to the ninth century the Greeks driven by the invaders had expanded from the mainland of Greece, as we know it today, and had colonized the shores of Asia Minor.

Greece in the eighth century was just emerging from three hundred years of darkness, but it was during this century that the Greeks began the renaissance of their artistic and cultural life which had been interrupted about the year 1100.

In the eighth century reasonably accurate historical dates begin, all reckoned from the first Olympic games in 776. Greek history from this time on becomes increasingly more factual than mythological. The Greeks turned their attention to the rich lands across the sea to the west and built their first city at Cumae, north of the later city of Neapolis (Naples) in Italy, about the year 750, although it is possible that the island of Ischia in the Bay of Naples was their first settlement.

They then turned to Sicily and founded Naxos on the eastern shore near the Strait of Messina. Shortly thereafter they settled in Syracuse, which was to become such a large and important city with a magnificent bay for the harboring of a fleet. The next step was to protect the passage of the Strait of Messina by building the cities of Rhegium (present-day Reggio) and Zancle (Messina) on either side of the waterway.

Scholars have generally placed the founding of Sybaris, lying in the arch of the Italian boot, at 720, a date deduced from writings of Strabo, Antiochus, and Pseudo Scymnus (see Dunbabin, page 24, cited in Bibliography). Pseudo Scymnus says the Sybarites had lived there 210 years before its destruction in 510.

Additional cities were established along the southern and western shores of Italy and in the eastern half of Sicily. These cities achieved great wealth and erected magnificent buildings and temples, many of which may be seen today. Along the coast as far away as southern France the Greek colonists settled, founding the city of Marseilles about 600. Cities were also established on the south coast of Spain.

Not content with this expansion to the west, a group of Greeks from Miletus in Asia Minor founded the city of Naucratis (ruler of the sea) in the year 650 at the mouth of the Nile, and went on to build a series of cities on the shores of present-day Libya.

Expansion was now at its crest. As early as the eighth century the Greeks had built many cities on the eastern shores of the Dardanelles, the Sea of Marmora, and all the way to the Bosporus. In 660 Byzantium was founded on the west coast, to become the present-day Constantinople. Having secured control of the Bosporus, they moved on to the Black Sea, which they called the Euxine, meaning "sea friendly to strangers," and about the year 600 they had cities dotted along the entire coast of this inland sea.

They now held dominion over the shores of the Mediterranean, except for the Phoenician coast at the eastern end and a part of the north coast of Africa, occupied by the Carthaginians. The coast of Italy north of Rome was the home of the Etruscans. This rich empire, extending from the Black Sea to the Straits of Gibraltar, was never unified in a single state. Though it was all Greek, a ship from one city could not be sure of the welcome it might receive on arriving at another port. Had all these different city states been able to live at peace with one another, the Greek Empire, instead of succumbing to the Romans, might have survived, to the advantage of all the world.

In comparison with later explorers such as Columbus, the voyages of the Greeks were relatively simple. The trip from Greece to Asia Minor was easily made by sailing from one island to the next. Even from Epirus on the west coast of Greece, the trip to Iapygia, the heel of Italy, was only a short distance, and the ships never had to be more than thirty miles from land. When storms approached, the sailors could run to the nearest shore and simply beach their boats.

Greece itself had no central government at this time but was made up of countless "poleis," or small city-states. Originally the polis was a small fort on a hill which came to be known as the "acropolis." As the king of the village became more powerful and the population expanded, the word "polis" was applied to all the territory ruled from the central acropolis. In the deep valleys of this mountainous country there was only a certain amount of fertile soil to support the growing polis, but for defense the inhabitants confined themselves to the valley, with the protection of the surrounding mountains.

Each polis became self-sufficient in its own arts and various crafts. They were usually located near enough to the seacoast that they traded with one another, the Aegean islands, and Asia Minor. Fighting between two poleis was constant, and more destruction was caused when Greek met Greek than in any foreign attacks. The male population was raised in the art of war. Sybaris itself, as we shall read, was destroyed by a neighboring city of Greeks who had migrated from Achaea, the original home of the Sybarites, and the most destructive Greek war, that between Athens and Sparta, lasted for twenty-seven years.

The colonies established throughout the Mediterranean were sometimes founded by two Greek poleis jointly. Sybaris was an example, the bulk of the settlers being Achaeans with a scattering of Troezenians. The relationship between a colony and the mother city was not as we think of it today. The Greeks never had our postwar problem of giving freedom to colonies which were completely untrained in self-government. From the beginning the colonies were independent, made their own laws, and paid no tribute to the mother city, and no "favored nation" clause existed in their trade. However, they did maintain a sentimental relationship and might call upon the homeland for help in time of war. This help was not always forthcoming. It depended largely on whether the mother polis had friendly relations with the adversary.

The colonies had to fend for themselves from the time of their founding, and practically all of them flourished. Trade brought great wealth. They imported goods from Asia Minor, and many Greek works of art and pottery are found in the modern excavations. There were large stands of timber in the virgin forests, and some colonies, such as Sybaris, presumably had silver mines.

The colonies did a thriving business supplying Greece with metals, principally iron and tin. The iron, mined on the island of Elba, was obtained from the Etruscans, who had set up a modern Pittsburgh on their coast. Tin came from as far as Cornwall in England, at that time a practically unknown country. Timber for the building of ships and the fine-quality wheat which they grew were sent to the homeland, deficient in both of these essentials. Wine and cattle contributed further to their revenues. At times, a certain amount of piracy added to their wealth, although there is no mention in the case of Sybaris of any ships belonging to the city. In spite of being on the sea and having ample wood available, the Sybarites apparently built no ships and had no navy. It is only in their successor city of Thurii that we read of sailors and a Thurian fleet.

# III

# SYBARIS

The founders of Sybaris were largely Achaeans who came from the city of Helice, the religious capital of Achaea, on the south shore of the Gulf of Corinth near its western end. They were accompanied, in the year 720, by a small band of Troezenians from the district of Argolis on the northeast coast of the Peloponnesus.[5] The physical surroundings of Helice were much like the plain of Sybaris, and it was built near the shore between the mouths of the rivers Selinus and Cerynites. A strange similarity to the fate of Sybaris overtook Helice, for it too disappeared completely about 372 as the result of an earthquake and tidal wave. There was not a single survivor of this catastrophe and, although for hundreds of years the ruins were to be seen under the sea,[6] today there is no trace left of this once great and prosperous city.*

* In the summer of 1966 the Greek Government asked the University Museum to send its instruments, with Elizabeth K. Ralph in charge, to help them locate the ruins of Helice. Unfortunately,

Is, of Helice, is credited with being the founder of Sybaris. He took his small sailing vessels along the magnificent coast of the Ionian Sea some four hundred miles from home. The largest of his ships may have had forty oars, but it was mainly the sails upon which he depended. As he rounded the heel of Italy, the Gulf of Taranto opened before him, its tideless shore ringed by superb beaches stretching for miles. The background of the Apennines must have appeared very similar to the land he and his companions had just left. No ancient author tells us why they sailed along the coast for a hundred miles before reaching the spot where they finally settled. Later cities were to be founded all along this shore, and it may be that the two rivers between which they built their city reminded them of Helice and that they therefore chose this as a propitious site. There was no bay or anchorage for ships along the beaches, and in those days the ships were drawn up on the beach much as small boats are today. The site of Sybaris is an overwhelmingly beautiful one: a rich and fertile plain bordering the sea for some twenty-four miles and extending eighteen miles inland to the mountains, which rise almost immediately from the plain to a height of seven thousand feet and dominate the coast. Not only was the land productive, but at that time the mountains were covered with forests. The plain is abundantly watered by the streams coming down from the melting snow. Shortly after this landing at Sybaris, the Achaeans also founded the city of Croton, about seventy miles to the west of Sybaris, in 710. At about the same time the city of Tarentum (present-day Taranto), which was to play an important part in the Punic Wars, was built at the eastern end of the Gulf of Taranto.

---

the work was not successful owing to the excessive magnetic matter in the area: iron grape arbors, wire mesh fences, and even bomb fragments.

With these and other cities the Greeks had firmly established themselves on the south shore of Italy, and controlled the Strait of Messina and the south and east coasts of Sicily.

At the time of the founding of Sybaris, the land was inhabited by a number of local tribes which had been there from prehistoric times. There were only two of these tribes with whom the Sybarites had direct contact, the Bruttians and the Lucanians, as the city was built close to the eastern border of the Bruttians, whose territory covered the toe of Italy. The Lucanians occupied a strip of land encompassing the arch and the west coast of the Gulf of Salerno.

Far to the north were the Etruscans, who inhabited the land north of Rome along the Ligurian Sea to present-day Pisa. The Etruscans were to play an important part in the life of Sybaris, whose trade with them was to add so much to the wealth of the Greek city.

The land of the Lucanians was almost entirely covered by the Apennines. Along the shore of the Ionian Sea to the south are many fertile valleys and coastal plains. In the south the torrents from the snow-covered mountains supply numerous streams which are extremely valuable in the cultivation of the land, but over the centuries so much soil has been washed down into the plain by constant floods that we believed Sybaris might lie at a depth of twenty to thirty feet below the surface. On the west coast, emptying into the Tyrrhenian Sea south of Naples, there is only one important river, the Sele, and it was near here that Sybarites built the city of Paestum, which they called Poseidonia, where the temples still standing give us a picture of what may be beneath the soil of the plain of Sybaris. Farther south on the west coast, they built Laus and Skidros as trading ports with the Etruscans. No trace of these cities remains.

When the Sybarites arrived in Italy, the native Lucanians

and Bruttians who had lived there since prehistoric times apparently welcomed them and allowed them to build their cities and use the land. This entire area was first called Oenotria, the name of a local tribe, by the Greeks and later came to be known as Magna Graecia as flourishing cities developed here and in Sicily.

Although there are no accounts of early difficulties in Magna Graecia, all could not have been plain sailing, for Herodotus[7] writes of another settlement of the Greeks at Miletus:

"As for those who came from the very town hall of Athens and deem themselves the best born of the Ionians, these did not bring their wives with them to their settlements, but married Carian women whose parents they had put to death. For this slaughter, these women made a custom and bound themselves by oath that none would sit at meat with her husband nor call him by his name, because the men had married them after slaying their fathers and husbands and sons."

Both the Bruttians and the Lucanians retained their freedom until the Romans subjugated them after they had given aid to Hannibal in the war with Carthage in 216. These people were not simple tribesmen, as they had developed their own cities and coinage and indeed were at the height of their power some five hundred years after the founding of Sybaris and for three centuries after its destruction.

# IV

# OFF TO SYBARIS

In June, 1962, when the first work of excavation was under way, my wife and I left Rome by train for Sybaris. At the station we met Fro Rainey, who had just come in from Egypt, where he had been working on the Nubian salvage campaign before the construction of the high dam.

Also on the train was Signor Lerici, a wiry and vital Italian who had personally invented and financed the instruments which had such great success in Tuscany. Now in his seventies, he was enthusiastically adding his knowledge to that of Fro's in the search for Sybaris, where his instruments had discovered the long wall. Fortunately, he spoke excellent English, as neither my wife, Susy, nor I spoke Italian. His men, he told us, were already at work with a portable drill he had supplied for the summer, and were sinking test holes wherever the instruments showed that there were objects beneath the surface. To complete our party was another Italian who spoke no English and, in fact, hardly spoke at all during the seven hours we were on the train.

I did not learn who he was until the next day, when he turned out to be the most important member of the trip. It was Professor Giuseppe Foti, the Superintendent of Antiquities for the Italian Government in Calabria, and the Museum party worked under his supervision. Permission to excavate could be obtained only through him, and his decision was final. Even if, in Dr. Rainey's opinion, a great discovery lay within reach, we could not dig an inch further unless Professor Foti believed it wise to do so.

The trip down by train was enchanting. In the first place, the Italian Pullman cars and service are far better than those in the United States. With ample room, and tables between each two seats, a delicious meal is served at one's seat, and the cars are remarkably smooth in their operation. The scenery from Naples to Paola, the small town where one disembarks for Sybaris, is superb. The line skirts the shore of the Tyrrhenian Sea with mountains never more than a few miles inland and often coming down to the sea where the railroad pierces them with a tunnel. Dotted along the summits of the foothills are the picturesque and ageless small towns of Italy. Leaving Naples, one passes through a land rich in historical significance for two and a half millennia. First the railroad runs between Vesuvius and the sea, where Pliny perished in attempting to rescue those who were being engulfed in the lava when the nearby city of Pompeii was destroyed. Shortly we came to the Gulf of Salerno where the American troops landed, and a few miles further is Paestum, that magnificent creation of the Sybarites. Beyond Paestum is Velia, the home of the Eleatic philosophers.

At Paola we were met by two small cars. One was driven by Signor Lerici's man, and from the other jumped out a very attractive young lady in her thirties, clad in khaki pants and a khaki jacket. This was Elizabeth K. Ralph, who was in charge of the work when Dr. Rainey was not there. For several years she has spent the summer months at Sybaris. With degrees in chemistry and physics, she has the official title of Associate Director of the Applied Science Center for Archaeology at the University of Pennsylvania. Her knowledge of the inner workings of electronics is invaluable in using the magnetometer, and to her must go a large amount of the credit for the rapid development of the instruments.

I learned later that she is the leading expert in this field and that she had been asked to assist in work in Israel, Greece, and Italy as well as other countries. Her experience as an All-American hockey star has given her the vigor needed in her work, for I have known her to spend long hours at the dig working with her assistants and then labor far into the night examining the data collected during the day.

In her laboratory at the University, she has developed a new method for dating pottery. The Carbon 14 method of dating is successful only on remains of matter containing carbon. Miss Ralph has used the "thermoluminescence" technique, which may most simply be described in the words of Dr. Rainey: "Radiation from minute traces of radioactive elements in pottery clay bombards other substances in the clay and raises electrons to slightly unstable levels. When the clay is fired in the kiln, each electron falls back to its stable position and emits a photon of light. When a fragment of pottery is reheated in the laboratory, the amount of thermoluminescence observed represents the accumulated radiation damage, and hence the time elapsed since the original firing of the pottery."

The discovery is indicative of Miss Ralph's brilliant mind, which has been of such value in the invention and development of the instruments used in the search for Sybaris.

*Beth Ralph*

A test on a superb Etruscan statuette at the University Museum, supposedly dating from 500 B.C., has proved it to be a forgery made in modern times. Undoubtedly her discovery will be of enormous value to collectors and museums in determining the authenticity of what they now own, and, even of more importance, it may deter the many modern artists who specialize in creating antique sculpture and pottery.

With Beth, as Fro called her, at the wheel, we began our trip. From the station the road twists and turns almost straight up the side of a mountain rising to over four thousand feet directly above the Tyrrhenian Sea. Beth told us that as you reach the top there is quite likely to be a heavy bank of clouds, so that you frequently are driving across the pass in a thick fog. Luckily none existed that day, and the view was superb. After crossing the mountain pass and descending gradually into the valley of the Crati River, we drove through a heavily wooded area with rich stands of enormous chestnut trees. Before us hillside towns came into view and the valley unfolded. Going through a small town, we came upon the only traffic lights on this route, where the main street of the town is so narrow that two cars cannot pass. There is a light at either end of the town, and traffic moves in one direction at a time while at the other end the oncoming traffic waits. The trick is not to be caught behind a cart drawn by oxen! The valley of the Crati is richly covered with cultivated fields, and pastures for the cattle reach well up the sides of the surrounding foothills.

We were now in the country settled by the Greeks in the eighth century, and there are many hidden reminders, evidence of this early period of civilization. Almost daily the plowman, slowly plodding behind his span of oxen, will turn up a piece of an ancient vase, a terracotta head, or the remains of an early metal lamp.

On the way we stopped for a brief visit at Cosenza, and I was able to see how right Dr. Rainey had been. Looking for Alaric in the river would have been just as productive as looking for him in the Seine in Paris. Instruments, aerial surveys, and even guesswork would have been hopeless in this river, which is now confined in a new course through a flourishing modern city, and whose old bed may lie under a present-day building. Our road continued along the Crati River and through the land of the Bruttians, the great tribe whose origins go back to prehistoric times.

With the sun at our backs, providing a beautiful golden light on the mountains, we skirted the edge of a hill and came in sight of the great plain of Sybaris. Before us were the Apennines rising several thousand feet, and to our right a flat expanse of land stretched ten or twelve miles to the shore of the Mediterranean. The first crops had been harvested, and the contrast of the golden yellow of the stubble of the wheat with the deep green of the alfalfa provided a scene worthy of the Impressionists. In a minute we were running alongside the banks of the fabled Sybaris River, perhaps one hundred yards apart at this point, but now, with the spring floods ended, only a small stream wound between them.

With the Sybaris on our left, we shortly saw a much larger and free-flowing river on our right. This was again the Crati, about which the ancient authors have much to tell us in relation to its proximity to Sybaris. The two rivers now join about three miles from the sea, the juncture being hidden by a small woodland rising above the fields. From all the ancient accounts which I had read, I felt that we were nearing the spot where the city would be located.

On either side of the road were small farms with spotless houses which had been built by the Government since the last war. Up until the time when the American troops were there, this whole plain was malarial and had lain uncultivated for many years. The Americans sprayed the area and eliminated the mosquitoes, and the richness of the soil is now available with no danger of illness. The fields are bordered by irrigation ditches with high banks on which poplar and eucalyptus trees have been planted as windbreaks. In a very few years, with their roots in the water, they have grown well and add much to the beauty of the farms. Oxen work in the fields with an occasional tractor, and the land is so rich that it is not unusual to get six crops of alfalfa a year without fertilizing. Orange trees flourish; also wheat and corn, rice, sugar beets, and melons are grown. From time to time we passed herds of cows going home for the milking.

We soon came to a railroad crossing flanked by an oblong white building with a single word, "SIBARI." Thoughts ran through my mind of all that this meant in terms of the past and what the future might hold for us. It was almost as though our trip were accomplished and we must find in the neighborhood of this romantic sign the city we were so hopeful of unearthing. The town of Sibari consists of a few houses strung along the road and one grocery store, which we were later to find would be the source of the fresh bread, wine, and cheese that made our daily lunch at the dig. There is a small local museum of antiquities where objects found around Sybaris are on display, if you can find the guardian to open the door for you. We continued on about five miles to Trebisacce, a town on the coast where we found a small, clean, modern hotel on the beach. Trebisacce is reputed to be the home of the tools used in the construction of the wooden horse of Troy, thus carrying its mythology back some three thousand years. However, this claim could be disputed by Metaponto (ancient Metapontum), for we have an account by Justinus that in the Temple of Minerva are the iron instruments with which Epeus constructed the Trojan horse.[8] We were charmed by our hotel room, looking out on the peaceful ocean, and directly beneath our window were the fishing boats drawn up on the beach, exactly as they had been twenty-five hundred years ago. A shower was in order after a long day, but unfortunately when I turned it on, the metal nozzle fell on my completely bald head, inflicting a neat little wound. Dinner was served on the terrace, and nothing could have been more romantic as the moon rose from the sea. We were looking forward to a good night's sleep, but we had not counted on the Italians' love of *conversazione*. The terrace below our window was the meeting

The White Oxen of Sybaris

place for the social life of the city, and voices, growing louder as the night progressed, kept up an animated discussion. It seemed as though we had barely gone to sleep before the fishermen returned well before dawn to beach their boats, and each boat had to be shouted at in different terms of abuse to persuade it to slide ashore. The next night we moved to the back of the hotel, thoroughly unromantic, but at least quiet.

# V

# EARLY DAYS OF
# SYBARIS

S o many ancient authors have mentioned the approximate place where the city of Sybaris may be in this great and bountiful plain that we felt we should narrow our first search to the areas of which they have spoken. Not one of the authors tells us whether the city lay inland or on the sea, but we did know that there was no bay or harbor mentioned. We also knew that it lay between two rivers, but which two was not definite.

Although over eighty such authors mention Sybaris or the successor city of Thurii, unfortunately we have no contemporary source. Many of the authors to whom I shall refer had the advantage of reading the accounts of even earlier historians whose works have since been lost. Scylax,[9] born in 521, eleven years before the fall of Sybaris, only mentions the rivers Sybaris and Crathis. The next earliest author is the great historian Herodotus, who was born in 484 and lived a large part of his life at nearby Thurii and died there. Although we know Thurii was built after the final destruction of Sybaris in the immediate neighborhood, it too has never been found and may offer great archaeological possibilities, although it would not compare with Sybaris either in richness or in historic interest. So much is told us about Sybaris that it was certainly no mythical city for which we were looking, but one which is fully recognized as having been of the first magnitude in Grecian life of the seventh century. Herodotus[10] begins by speaking of the name of the Crathis River, which was taken from the never-failing river of this same name at Aegae. Another reference is Pausanias in his *Description of Greece*,[11] who tells us of the river Crathis, as well as the mountain of the same name where the river had its source, and says that this river gave its name to the Crathis in Italy. To impress upon us its importance as well as his accuracy, he again says,[12] "Shortly after passing the sanctuary of the Pythian Apollo you will be on the road that leads to Mt. Crathis. On this mountain is the source of the river Crathis, which flows into the sea by the side of Aegae, now a deserted spot, though in earlier days it was a city of the Achaeans. After this Crathis is named the river in Bruttium in Italy." So much for the Crathis, and we now come to the Sybaris. Pseudo Scymnus[13] mentions the city as well as the river in these words, "there was once also a greatly celebrated large city, austere, opulent, beautiful, named from the Sybaris river." Dionysius of Halicarnassus, in his *Roman Antiquities*,[14] says that "Croton is a city in Italy, likewise Sybaris, so named for the river which flows past it."

Though other ancient authors tell us of these rivers, not one of them says whether the city lay at the mouth of the river or whether it is inland. In addition to this it is unquestionably a fact that in those days each of the rivers had its own outlet to the sea, whereas the modern Coscile—which may be the ancient Sybaris, as there is no river of this name today—flows into the Crati at a point several miles inland. Strabo, in his *Geography*, makes several references to the location of Sybaris and, in speaking of Myscellus, the founder of neighboring Croton, he says,[15] "but when he saw that Sybaris was already founded . . . having the same name as the river nearby." He then goes on to locate the city most definitely[16] as being between two rivers, the Crathis and the Sybaris. Another author, Diodorus,[17] confirms this statement that the city was between two rivers. Finally, the only other reference we have is from Athenaeus, who wrote in his *Deipnosophistae*[18] that the Sybarites "prided themselves in their turn on having grown to old age at the bridges of their two rivers" and[19] further helps us by pointing out that the city was not built in the hills: "Their city lying, as it does, in a hollow."

From these various authors we were able to assume that the search for Sybaris should logically begin on the plain and in a position between the two rivers at some point where there might have been bridges. There were two difficulties in making any dogmatic statement about the site. It is unquestionably true that during the course of twenty-five hundred years the rivers have changed their courses, and there is also the question of the name of the Sybaris River. It is accepted practice today to consider that the modern Coscile is the ancient Sybaris, lying north of the Crati, whose name remains the same as in ancient times. However, there are certain authorities who question whether the former Sybaris River is not the San Mauro, which lies to the south of the Crati. Therefore, although we presumably knew that Sybaris lay near the Crati, it might be either to the north or south of this river.

There was, however, one other complication in a brief passage in Athenaeus[20] which reads, "since the sea which stretches beside it affords no harbor." He was writing several hundred years after the destruction of Sybaris, but he did have access to the works of Timaeus, which, except for some fragments, have since been lost. It is possible that Timaeus, who lived in the fourth century B.C., might have seen the ruins of Sybaris. This sentence, in conjunction with the one that says,[21] "most of them own wine cellars near the seashore, into which the wines are sent through pipes from their country estates; part of it is sold outside the country, part of it, again, is carried to the city in boats," gives a clue which the archaeologist cannot overlook, and justifies him in looking for the city near the coast, as well as further inland. The only question here is why, if the city was near the seashore, the inhabitants had separate wine cellars also near the shore. Some later authors believed there were canals leading from the sea to the inland city. None of the wine pipes leading to the sea has yet been found.

In addition to the enormous amounts of soil which now may lie from ten to thirty feet deep over the foundations of the former city, the problem was further complicated by the fact that the water table in this plain lies only about six feet below the present surface, so that anyone excavating is faced with the difficulty of keeping the water out of the pit which is dug.

The sight of the rich and fertile valley at Sybaris, together with the magnificent forests on the mountains, must have worked on the imagination of the Achaeans much as the plains of the American West did to the pioneers of the nineteenth century. Here was a new and abundant life offered to them in place of the restricted and overpopulated land which they had left, and the country was even similar in appearance to the home which had been theirs. They promptly gave names to the two major rivers which were the same as those they had used in Greece. The Sybaris spring was located in Greece near the mother city of Helice, and the Crati (the spelling of this river varies and is Crati, Crathis, or Crathi) was so called after the river in Achaea, which received its original name owing to its being a mixture of two rivers.[22] There has never been any historical question of the names of these rivers, as they are mentioned by so many of the ancient authors.[23] After a few years of living by these rivers, the Sybarites attributed special qualities to them. Ovid[24] mentions the numerous fish in the Crati, while several other authors mention miraculous qualities: The Sybaris was reported to make those who drink it timorous, and therefore the horses were kept away from it.[25] The Crati would turn them white,[26] and those who drink of the Sybaris are darker and hardier—which seems a direct contradiction of their being timorous—with curly hair, while those who drink of the Crati are fair, softer, with straight hair.[27] Although it is possible to imagine certain qualities of these streams, it is hard to accept the statement that Athenaeus attributes[28] to Metagenes: "The river Crati brings down for us huge barley cakes which have kneaded themselves, while the other river thrusts its billow of cheese cakes and meat and boiled rays wriggling to us here." The Greek gods did wondrous things in those days, and from Homer to Thucydides we can read of the miracles which happened to turn the tide of battle.

We also have written evidence of the fruitfulness of this valley and the bountiful living that it was to provide the new settlers. The countryside is described as being extensive and fruitful and bringing great riches to the inhabitants.[29] The land in the spring was aglow with the whiteness of the wheat,[30] and the normal yield from the wheat seed was 100 to 1.[31] Game abounded, and partridge was so plentiful that a group of Samians were frightened from the shore and sailed away when they heard the drumming of the partridge wings.[32]

The vineyards were to become famous and the wine among the best which was pressed in Italy.[33] Between the rows of vines the Sybarites grew cabbages, which aided in producing a darker wine, and they used to eat cabbage before drinking.[34] They were evidently careful in their making of the wine, as the grapes were not harvested until there had been a frost.[35]

The valleys provided ample pasture for the cattle, horses, sheep, and goats which they raised, and the bull's head became the symbol which was stamped on the coins of Sybaris. The heads of the oxen of today show a strong resemblance to those on the coins of twenty-five hundred years ago. The wool produced was probably not of the finest quality, for there is mention of the importation of the famous Milesian wool from Asia Minor.

At that time the abundant forests on the mountains were not only of use in the building of houses, but also of great value for exportation and for the building of ships. As I have mentioned, there is no record that Sybaris ever developed a navy or merchant ships, which would have seemed natural to a maritime race, and one which depended for much of its prosperity on trade between the Middle East and the west coast of Italy.

It is apparent that the location of this great city was ideal for the sustenance of a large and growing population, and it is easy to visualize how this fertile territory could serve as a base for the development of a trade which was to make Sybaris a byword for riches and luxury. Some historians have claimed that Sybaris, both in population and wealth, was greater than Athens even in the later Periclean age, but it does not seem pertinent to form any exact comparison. It is evident from all the ancient accounts that Sybaris was considered to be one of the greatest and most prosperous of Greek cities and was devoted to a life of ease and luxury

*Paestum*

far exceeding that of its rivals. We also have the example of the temples which the Sybarites built when they established Poseidonia (present-day Paestum) on the west coast of Italy south of Salerno. The three temples, still standing, are perfect examples of the architecture of the sixth, fifth, and fourth centuries, and one of them, that of Neptune, has been described by Sestieri as without doubt the most beautiful and most perfect of Doric temples. If these temples were built by the people of Sybaris in a smaller city, constructed for the purposes of trade, how great may be the treasure which has lain for so many centuries under the soil of the plain of Sybaris? Of course, it is too much to hope that standing temples will still be found, as there have probably been earthquakes and soil subsidence over the years, but the ruins must still be there and, possibly, unforeseen masterpieces of sculpture. Herodotus, who was born only twenty-six years after the destruction of the city and was living nearby, says,[36] "The Sybarites show a precinct and a temple beside the dry bed of the Crathis." This is as close as we can come to direct contemporary evidence that there were buildings on the banks of the river. Perhaps the best summation of the reason for the long and painstaking search for Sybaris which has been undertaken by archaeologists of many nations for over a hundred years is contained in the words of that great authority on the Western Greeks, T. J. Dunbabin, who says, "Perhaps some day the wealth and skill needed for its discovery will be united, to produce the richest and most valuable reward which a Greek archaeologist can imagine."

We can picture a small group of Achaeans, with a few Troezenians, establishing some form of temporary village in this great plain, near the rivers and possibly, at the outset, close to the Ionian Sea. When they later founded Paestum (I use the modern name), we know that they first built the city near the sea and surrounded it with fortifications, but later moved it inland.[37] Did they do the same at Sybaris? That is a question that has puzzled archaeologists, and the accounts remaining to us were not sufficiently clear to warrant a judgment. All that we knew definitely was that it lay in a hollow[38] and was between two rivers.[39] Unless the whole plain is considered "a hollow," there is no great valley until one reaches the foothills of the Apennines, and then the city could not have been near the two rivers, for their courses do not approach each other until they have reached the plain. However, there are two small hills jutting out into the plain, and it is possible to consider the land between them as being in a hollow. In olden days the rivers Sybaris, Crati, and San Mauro all reached the sea at separate mouths, but

today the Coscile (if that is the Sybaris of old) joins the
Crati about three miles from the Mediterranean. Shortly
after the settlement the Achaeans drove out the Troezenians
who had come with them; this was the first of the acts
which brought upon them the wrath of the gods who were
to acquiesce in their later destruction.[40] At the same time
the people of Sybaris were plotting with their neighbors and
fellow Achaeans from Metapontum to drive out the other
Greeks in Italy,[41] for they found the land so rich that they
were endeavoring to control its later development. In studying their conquests, one should remember that it was not
the natives with whom they were fighting, but fellow Greeks
and often their own brother Achaeans who were establishing rival cities.

In all probability it was forty or fifty years before the
final city of Sybaris took form. By that time the population
had increased enormously, and there are various estimates
which place the size of the city at 300,000.[42] Other authors
are more conservative and give the population as 100,000;[43]
even this was a very large city for those times.

However, all this should be taken with several grains
of salt, and the figures may very well refer to the whole area
which the city controlled. For we know[44] that they encouraged immigration and granted citizenship to the newcomers,
so that in the seventh century the horde of immigrants who
had heard of this rich and bountiful land must have been
very similar to the tide of Europeans who came to America
in the nineteenth century. In any case they constructed a city
whose walls had a circumference of fifty stadia (five and a
half miles; the walls of Athens, built by Themistocles, had
a circumference of about this size), and they were then ruling
over four tribes of the original inhabitants and had twenty-
five subject cities.[45]

# VI

# SYBARIS IN 600 B.C.

We have no accurate account of what Sybaris may have looked like, and it is only by piecing together what is said about other Greek cities that we may try to draw a picture of this opulent metropolis. As it is constantly described as having been the richest and most luxurious of all, it is reasonable to base our image of Sybaris in 600 on what we read of this and somewhat later periods. None of what I am now writing is based on an account of the actual city, but is a compendium of information on the life of the period.

We will presume that the city lies on this flat plain surrounded by strong walls made of large blocks of stone socle at the base with a mud-brick superstructure. The walls are at least twelve feet thick at the base and upward of thirty feet high with a flat top for the use of the defenders in time of siege. Running east and west, the city is about one mile long, and the north and south walls are two miles long. In the center of each wall is a gate, fortified by towers, with other towers at intervals along the wall. Through the city from each of these gates runs a wide paved street, leading to the main country roads at the four points of the compass. Within the city most of the other streets are narrow, unpaved, and have no sidewalks, and many of them are no more than winding alleys, dusty in summer and muddy in winter. At the center of the city where the two main streets meet is the agora, or public square. This is a large open space which serves many purposes. It is a gathering place for all sorts of festivals and meetings, and along one side is a primitive stoa, or colonnade. The stoa is two stories high with Doric columns supporting the upper story and a similar row of columns rising to the roof, which is covered with brightly colored tiles. Along the roofline are statues of the gods. In the back of the stoa, facing the covered walk, are luxury shops. This stoa provides a shady spot for strolling and conversation and is protected completely from the weather, but has three sides fully open to the air. Opposite the stoa is the building housing the law courts, and on the other sides are the city hall and the treasury. On certain days of the week movable market booths are brought into the agora, and it then becomes a busy and active place, very similar to the market days in the main squares of European cities today. Parades and spectacles also take place in the agora. Along the tops of all the buildings are magnificent statues in the archaic style. The beauty, comfort, and pleasure of the agora are enhanced by the planting of shade trees, and on two sides are fountains with water flowing freely, where the slaves come to fill their jars.

Turning away from the agora and going out a wide street to the north, we come to the magnificent Temple of Poseidon, god of the sea, built in the Doric style with the sculpture and carvings painted in bright colors. This is one of the earliest temples of the Greeks and is even larger than its namesake at present-day Paestum. On this same street is another stoa, even longer than the one in the agora, and along this street are many of the houses of the wealthy. Going west along the bisecting avenue, we see a smaller Temple to Apollo, and not far from it is the Gymnasium, a vast complex with stone-columned rooms which are used for boxing, wrestling, and ball playing. There is also an open-air space where discus-throwing, spear-throwing, running, and jumping are practiced by the naked Sybarite youths. In the Gymnasium there are also rooms for more sedentary games such as dice and backgammon. It is the custom for the older men to meet here as well as in the stoas for gossip and philosophical discussions. Most of their life is lived out of doors in the streets and the columned buildings.

Along this street are the public baths, which are much frequented by the more well-to-do citizens. Nearby are barber shops, which are also busy, not only with hairdressing and beard trimming, but also with conversation where all the latest news is passed from one to another.

In one of the smaller streets behind the Gymnasium is an old wooden Temple of Hera, the earliest in the city, built not long after its settlement, about the year 700.

Going east from the agora, we come to the shopping district, where the artisan, who has made his wares at his home outside the walls (for no noisy manufacturing is allowed within the city walls), displays them in small stores which occupy the street fronts of the larger houses. Here also are the stores containing the goods imported from foreign lands, the magnificent pottery of Athens and Corinth, the Milesian woolens, the jewels, gold and silver goblets and platters, necklaces, bracelets, and dyes. On the smaller streets we find produce, fish, and poultry being sold. At the far end of the street, near the city wall, is an open space for the theater. This is extremely simple and consists solely of a raised wooden platform for the actors, benches for the citizens, and standing room for the rest of the population. It was not until long after the days of Sybaris that the magnificent stone and marble theaters which we think of in connection with the Greeks were built in Greece and the colonies.

Near the southern gate of the city is a slight rise in the land which provides a place for assembly where the citizens meet to discuss the laws and foreign policy. Here there is a small stone platform for the speaker, and we are now looking at that which is called the Bema.

Leaving the city through the north gate, we find the Sybaris River running slowly by the city walls, and we cross on one of the two bridges to the farms and the country estates of the more affluent. The road to the surrounding hills is tree-lined, and the farther we go from the city the richer are the houses until we get to the foothills where there are superb villas with views of the plain and the distant Ionian Sea. The farms are intensely cultivated, with cattle, sheep, and horses dotting the fields. The slopes of the hills are covered with grapevines.

If we go out the south gate, we cross the bridge of the swiftly flowing Crathis River, and quickly are in the midst of a small village where the tradesmen are busy making the goods which they sell in the city. Farther out this road lie the cemeteries.

The east gate of the city leads to the sea and the huts of the fishermen who supply so much of the food of the city. Here we are on the busy road of the port, where carts and porters bring in the riches that are imported from Greece and Asia Minor, part to be sold in the city, but the major portion to be put into warehouses for shipment, as caravans are made up, to Laus, Skidros, and Paestum where the cargo is put aboard the ships of the Etruscans.

Not far outside the western gate is an early type of stadium where the athletes meet. The pentathlon, in which each contestant takes part in five events—wrestling, running, jumping, discus-throwing, and javelin hurling—is the principal contest, which brings the winner a crown of olive leaves. Unfortunately, few of our athletes from Sybaris have been successful at the great Olympic games in Greece.

From the thousands of paintings on Greek vases we can see a vivid picture of the verve of the athlete. How different is the vigorous action shown in Greek painting from the stylized and formal work of the Egyptians. The Greeks believed in the beauty of the body and were not ashamed of it, and at these games the participants were naked, although few of the cities followed the example of the Spartans, where it is believed the girls also took part in the sports naked. Some of the finest sculpture was of athletes; the discus-thrower of Myron is known to all and the bronze of the prize fighter in the Baths of Diocletian in Rome is a marvelous example not only of sculpture, but of the superb physique of the man as he sits in a relaxed mood apparently listening to the words of his trainer. In the Museum of Athens is the statue of Poseidon in the attitude of throwing a spear. It would be hard to equal this for vivid action and a magnificent depiction of the male.

Most of the houses in the city are made of brick or wood, mainly of one story in height, although some of the larger dwellings and the public buildings are of two floors, built of stone.

On the houses of the wealthy citizens the façades are richly decorated. The outer gates to the house are usually open, and the great inner door may have a purple curtain which is let down when the door is open. Entering the portico, one comes upon a wide passage with doors on either side opening into small rooms. This hallway leads to an inner courtyard, which is surrounded by a peristyle affording protection against both sun and rain. In the center is a handsomely carved cistern to collect the rain water for the use of the household. The walls of this courtyard and of some of the larger rooms have wainscoting which is inlaid with gold and ivory. Above this there are brightly painted frescoes, giving the whole a gay and opulent effect. The floors are of marble or mosaic, and to admit light the windows are glazed with thin slabs of gypsum or talc. For protection the windows have superbly wrought bronze lattices, or intricate designs of wood and iron. The blinds are made either of leather or haircloth. The beams of the ceiling are painted in variegated colors. The roof is covered with large clay tiles, many of which we were later to find.

Within the house the furniture is sparse. There are chairs and stools, and along the walls are divans richly upholstered with fine materials and piled with cushions in various colors. The tables are both four- and three-legged, and if of wood are inlaid with ivory. Some are of solid silver. In the earlier times, before the days of divans, the Greeks ate at oblong tables and sat as we do in chairs.

When the walls are not painted, they are hung with Milesian tapestries, and the floors may have carpets of this famous wool. The lamps, both the small and standing ones, are often either bronze or silver and even gold. The mirrors are brightly polished bronze and silver, and in some houses there are chandeliers hanging from the beams of the ceilings. In the bedrooms the beds are made of wood inlaid with ivory. (In later days even silver beds were known.) The frames are strung with oxhide thongs, the mattresses stuffed with grass.

(Subsequently they had mattresses of sponge, thus anticipating our foam rubber by some twenty-five hundred years.) Their blankets are of wool, and they also have covers filled with down. The blankets and pillows are all perfumed.

Another passage leads to a second courtyard smaller than the first. Here are the workrooms and the larders, and from this court there is a staircase to the second floor, where there are additional bedrooms. In this court is a room for baths, and it is not unusual for the rich Sybarite to bathe four or five times a day and to be rubbed with oil at the conclusion of the bath. Unfortunately, the slaves never have an opportunity to bathe, which may explain the need for perfume. The slaves of the household have no rooms, but sleep in recesses in the walls near the doors of their masters.

Who knows but there may be one of these houses complete with its furnishings still buried beneath the soil of the plain of Sybaris? What a picture it would give us of this period of Greek life.

This luxury is possible only with extreme wealth and an abundant supply of slaves. We have mention of owners of one thousand or more slaves. These are used not only in the house but also as artists, carpenters—in fact, every type of workman. They labor on the farms, and a rich owner also leases them to his neighbors or to the mines, thus increasing his wealth. The slaves may be other Greeks who have been captured in one of the many wars between cities, or they may have been purchased from slave traders who have kidnaped them from Asia Minor and the southern coasts of the Black Sea. The owner exercises the power of life and death over his slaves; he can torture and beat them with impunity. On some occasions a faithful slave is given his freedom, but this does not entitle him to citizenship. (In later days the Athenians passed laws ameliorating the lot of the slave and even allowing him to sue the master for assault and battery. The slave was also able to purchase his freedom, but this was a long task, as his small earnings had to be accumulated over many years.) There were also slaves of the city and of the temples.

Although the well-to-do whom we meet in the street are dressed in rich and colorful materials, the design is comparatively simple. It consists in the case of the women of a long gown which is an oblong piece of material draped around the body. This is gathered above the waist with a girdle and in most cases, even when gathered, trails the ground. Over this they wear a shorter robe of rich colors, and in colder weather there is a magnificent cloak, often of purple embroidered with gold, which is thrown over the shoulders. Athenaeus[46] describes the luxury of these garments as "violet dyed, crimson and yellow woven in a lozenge pattern; but the top borders are marked at equal intervals with animal patterns." There are also robes dyed with quince yellow and sea purple; long robes from Corinth, flame color and sea green; and garments from Persia strewn with gold beads. The purple is considered a color rare even for princes. Over their heads the women wear a white veil, and their feet are encased in sandals which are of white satin and gold. They also have slippers of white satin embroidered with flowers, and the use of high heels of cork is prevalent. In the evenings they wear a variety of earrings of gold and precious stones, necklaces of pearls, and gold collars. Their fingers are laden with rings of gold and precious stones. Their hair is worn in curls over the shoulders, is sometimes dyed to a blond color, and is confined by a golden fillet. Much time is spent in its preparation and the use of cosmetics on the face. They use powder for the teeth, black paint for the eyebrows, rouge, and white powder. Over all is the aroma of their various perfumes. In fact, little has changed in the ladies' toilet from that day to this. Athenaeus[47] assures us that they "rubbed cosmetic on their faces and assumed false fronts attached to their hair."

The men we meet are clad in a similar straight garment, but in their case the short tunic is worn underneath and over this a cloak is thrown over one shoulder, leaving the spear arm free. The men's clothes are also richly dyed. In cold weather an outer coat of skins is worn. Many of them[48] "progressed to such a point of luxury as to have their entire bodies made smooth." On their feet they wear either Persian half-boots or sandals. They wear various rings on their fingers. Their hair is long and curled above the brow, and older men have beards; but in time of war the hair is close cropped so that a helmet can be easily adjusted.

Let us now join them, uninvited, at one of their evening meals. We will be well received, for often a friend passing by will drop in if he knows that a banquet is in progress. The cooks will have been informed from what parts of the world the guests will come so that they can prepare the regional specialty which will please an especially honored friend. The guests who arrive from a distance are bathed in the house of the host before dinner, and those with beards have them dressed and perfumed by the slaves. As we enter the dining room, we are struck by the beauty of the silver, the inlaid tables, and the richness of the cushions on the sofas which line the walls. In the center of the room is an altar upon which libations are poured to Zeus before the meal begins. This evening there are only about a dozen men present, and the talk is given over to philosophical conversation. We eat, of course, with our fingers and wash our hands in gold bowls at the end of every course. After dinner our host orders the tables removed, and we are then provided with music and singers. After this there is conversation over some of the good local wine before a different type of entertainment is forthcoming. This consists of jugglers, buffoons, monkeys, and acrobatic dancers. We are approaching the early morning hours, and the entertainers have left us. It is now that we engage in the true entertainment of the mind and, over the wine, a philosophical discussion is carried on until the sun is rising from the still waters of the Mediterranean.

This was a small and intimate dinner, and I cannot do better, in order to give you a picture of a more elaborate banquet, than quote the description[49] of the wedding feast of Caranus. In the usual marriage ceremony the bridegroom and his best man go in a carriage to the home of the bride. He returns with her to his parents' home, where he carries her over the threshold. Hesiod, in the *Shield of Heracles*,[50] gives an account of this:

"The men were making merry with festivities and dances; some were bringing home a bride to her husband on a well-wheeled car, while the bridal song swelled high, and the glow of blazing torches held by handmaidens rolled in waves afar. And these maidens went before, delighting in the festival; and after them came frolicsome choirs, the youths singing soft mouthed to the sound of shrill pipes, while the echo was shivered around them, and the girls led on the lovely dance to the sound of lyres."

Euripides, in *Helen*,[51] gives a brief and poetic account of this rite:

"Now I recall afresh thy spousal tide
And how I waved the torch in four horsed car
Racing beside thee; and thou chariot borne
With him, a bride, didst leave thine happy home."

The wedding feast of Caranus is described in a letter from Hippolochus,[52] one of the guests, and reads substantially as follows:

"Caranus celebrated his marriage with a banquet at which the number of men invited to gather was twenty; no sooner had they taken their places on the couches, than they were presented with silver cups, one for each, to keep as their own. Each guest had been crowned before he entered with a gold tiara. And after they had emptied their cups, they were each given a bronze platter containing a loaf as wide as the platter; also chickens and ducks, and ring doves too, and a goose and an abundance of such viands piled high; and each guest took his portion, platter and all, and distributed among the slaves who stood behind him. Following which came a second platter of silver, on which again lay a huge loaf, and geese, hares, young goats and curiously moulded cakes besides, pigeons, turtle doves, partridges and other fowl in plenty. This also they presented to the slaves, and when they had had enough food they washed their hands. Then numerous chaplets were brought in, made of all kinds of flowers, and in addition gold tiaras, equal in weight to the first chaplet. Then they proceeded to drinking toasts and when they had at last pleasantly taken leave of all sobriety, there entered flute girls and singers and some Rhodian Sambuca players. The girls looked quite naked, but some said they had on tunics. Then came in other girls carrying each two jars fastened together with a gold band and containing perfume; one jar was silver, the other gold, and held half a pint. These also they gave to each guest. After that there was brought in a fortune rather than a dinner, namely a silver platter gilded all over to no little thickness, and large enough to hold a whole roast pig—a big one too—which lay on its back upon it. Roasted inside it were thrushes, ducks and warblers in unlimited number, peas puree poured over eggs, oysters and scallops; all of which towering high, was presented to each guest, platters and all. After this they drank, and then received a kid, piping hot, again upon a platter as large as the last, with spoons of gold. Caranus then ordered baskets and bread racks made of plaited ivory strips to be given the guests to contain their gifts. Then more crowns again, and a double jar of gold and silver containing perfume, equal in weight to the first. Then trooped in men, Ithyphallic dancers, clowns and some naked female jugglers who performed tumbling acts among swords, and blew fire from their mouths. After they had finished their attention was given to a warm and almost neat drink of three wines and very large gold cups were given each guest. After this draught they were all presented with crystal platters about two cubits in diameter, lying in a silver receptacle and full of a collection of all kinds of baked fish. Then they washed their hands again and put on crowns, again receiving gold tiaras twice the size of the former ones, and another double jar of perfume.

"They then each drank a six-pint bowl of Thasian wine and after this a chorus of one hundred entered singing tunefully a wedding hymn (for this was a marriage feast); then came in dancing girls, some attired as Nereids, others as Nymphs. They then threw open the room, which had been curtained all about with white linen, and when this curtain was drawn back it disclosed Cupids, Dianas, Pans and Hermae holding lights in silver brackets. While admiring this artistic device, boars were served to each guest, on silver platters rimmed with gold; they were skewered with silver spears. The slaves then stuffed their happy baskets full until the customary signal for concluding the banquet was sounded on the trumpet. After more drinking in small cups there came in the concluding courses; that is dessert in ivory baskets, and flat cakes of every variety. Then they arose and took leave, quite sober—the gods be their witness!—because they were apprehensive for the safety of the wealth they took with them. They had carried away a fortune from Caranus's banquet and were now looking for houses, or lands, or slaves to buy."

It seems extraordinary that in all the descriptions that we have of the life of Sybaris we find no mention of any intellectual life; in fact, we are told that they devoted their energy and thought to delicate living, sloth, and extravagance and knew little of other matters.[53] There is no account of any philosophical discussion, no artist or sculptor is mentioned, and not a single line of literature is attributed to a Sybarite. They imported their architects and lawgivers and even sought the help of others to lead their army. All this is in sharp contrast to other cities in Magna Graecia and must lead one to the conclusion that mental or physical activity was abhorrent to them. The city was evidently divided between an upper and a lower class, with none of the leaven provided by the middle class which might furnish leaders in government, the arts, and academic fields. New blood did not come to the top, and the ruling class was not able to provide the example necessary to prevent the dissolution and downfall of the city.

Slavery was one of the contributing factors in this dissolute life. Practically all unskilled labor and much of the skilled work was done by slaves. However, in the arts and crafts much of the work was done by the citizens, but we have no great examples of Sybaritic art, and much of the pottery and jewelry was imported from Greece, mainly from Athens and Corinth. The slaves, as a whole, were well treated, and we read that some critics complained of the opulence of the slaves and that they were often better off economically than the poorer classes of free men.

# VII

# THE ANCIENT
# ACCOUNTS

That the city was ruled in a manner to give the rich citizens every possible luxury and to spare them any inconvenience is well documented. The first law which they enforced was the one of quiet within the city, for they forbade any craft which produced noise. No blacksmiths, carpenters, and the like were allowed to disturb the sleep of the citizens. They did not even permit poultry to be kept for fear that the sound of the roosters would be too loud.[59] Their banquets, and indeed the daily table, were given much thought and care, and a cook who was especially famous would receive a crown.[55] If a cook were to invent a particularly felicitous new dish, it was his privilege to be the only one allowed to produce it for a period of one year; in this way they hoped to encourage others to make similar inventions and to establish a rivalry between their chefs which would redound to the fame of the host.[56] Perhaps this is one of the earliest recorded examples of the granting of a patent. They were slaves to their bellies and lovers of food and wine, and we are told[57] that

59

such was their devotion to luxury that they even preferred to
associate with the Ionians and Tyrrhenians because they
found that the Ionians surpassed all other Greeks in the extravagance of their lives and similarly the Tyrrhenians (by
which they were probably referring to the Etruscans) led a
more luxurious life than others in that region. A delightful
story is told of a Sybarite who once visited Sparta, which city
has been known for its stern, rigorous, and hardy life. When
this particular Sybarite returned from his visit, he told his
friends that he used to wonder at the bravery of the Spartans
but that after reclining on their wooden benches to eat with
them and witnessing what a frugal and utterly miserable life
they led, he could only conclude that they were no better
than the lowest of men, and that the most cowardly Sybarite
would choose to die rather than endure a life like theirs.[58]

We have read how their banquets were planned to give
time for ample preparation. As they were the first to invite
women to these public celebrations, they passed a law that
those who issued an invitation to a banquet should do so a
year in advance in order that the women might prepare their
dresses and other adornments in a manner in keeping with the
occasion and the long time provided.[59] What a pity that the
dressmakers of Paris and Rome were still in a barbarous state.
Probably at that time the rivalry in dress was just as great, but
at least there was little opportunity for two matrons to meet
wearing the same dress. It was quite a shocking innovation
for the women to attend[60] the formerly all-male dinners, and
we are told that in adorning themselves, regulations for the
use of cosmetics, depilatories, and so forth were drawn up
for them by Hemitheon.[61] They were extremely partial to
having Maltese puppies as playthings,[62] and at banquets they
would reward with golden crowns the men who were considered worthy to receive such honors, their names being

published at the State sacrifices and games. Regretfully, I must say that reference seems to apply principally to those who had supplied the gourmet attractions.[63] One delicate touch was their invention of the chamber pot, which we are told they carried to their drinking parties.[64] In all things they seem to have been able to reach the heights—or depths—of laziness!

In preparation for these banquets the true Sybarites spent an inordinate amount of time in bathing and perfuming themselves. They devised the tub for baths[65] and also lay in the enjoyment of vapor baths some twenty-five hundred years before the sauna became a popular form of relaxation in this country. In the bringing in of constant supplies of hot water for their tubs, they arranged that the water carriers and bath attendants should have shackles on their feet to prevent them from moving too fast and by their carelessness possibly scalding their masters.[66] In order to rationalize their gluttony and their wine-drinking, they evolved a theory that since the city lay in a hollow and in the daytime was intolerably hot, although cool in the morning and evening, it contributed greatly to their health to hold these drinking bouts.[67] They had a saying that anyone in Sybaris who did not wish to die before his allotted time must look neither upon the rising or setting sun. (This may also have been considered a preventive of malaria, which was later to ravage this plain and make it uninhabitable.) One Sybarite boasted that for twenty years he had not seen the sun rise or set, and this he regarded as something great and a remarkable testimony to his wealth.[68]

Some idea of this wealth will be gained by the story of Smindyrides, who was one of the richest of the Sybarites, and who was described by Herodotus as the most luxurious liver of his day. The tyrant of Sicyon, Cleisthenes by name, after winning a famous chariot race, made a proclamation that his daughter was to be married and that any suitor for her hand should come to his house. The daughter, Agarista, is described in glowing terms and was considered a girl of great beauty, charm, and accomplishment. Smindyrides decided to become a suitor and left Sybaris in a ship of fifty oars, all the rowers being his own slaves.

We are told[69] that he brought with him one thousand cooks and a similar number of bird catchers and also one thousand fishermen. It is a little difficult to accept this as other than a violent stretch of the imagination, since his own ship had only fifty oars. Arriving at Sicyon, he outshone, in his equipage, not only the other suitors, but even the tyrant himself, who, together with the whole city, was participating in the occasion. At the banquet which was held after his arrival, when a certain man approached Smindyrides to recline beside him at the table, Smindyrides remarked that he was here seeking the bride and that he intended to recline either with her or by himself.[70]

In the matter of clothes and jewelry the Sybarites were equally fastidious. Their woolen garments were made into tunics of gay and variegated colors, and at the waist they wore costly sashes and came to be called the "sash-tunics" by their neighbors in distinction from those who did not wear belts and were called "non-sash-tunics."[71] In small matters of this kind the Sybarites were proudly affecting an extravagant style which in their opinion would set them above their neighbors. Snobbishness, it would seem, can be traced back to the earliest of historical times, and the rich have always sought means of attempting to increase their self-importance by the display of wealth rather than intellect.

The Sybarites, not satisfied with the local wool or the product of their own looms, imported the then most famous woolen materials, which came from Miletus on the coast of

Asia Minor, and it was with this city that the city of Sybaris developed a large and friendly commercial relationship. The feeling was so strong that at the time of the destruction of Sybaris the Milesians, both young and old, shaved their heads and made great public lamentation and mourning, and according to Herodotus no two cities were ever so closely joined in friendship.[72] Unfortunately, the surviving Sybarites do not seem to have reciprocated when the Milesians themselves later suffered a defeat.

Aleisthenes has found his notch in history solely by the purchase of a cloak of a material so expensive and magnificent that he not only wore it, but even put it on display at Lacinium during the festival of Hera at which great throngs of Greeks gathered. It was the most admired object at the festival and later was owned by Dionysius the Elder, who in turn sold it to the Carthaginians for 120 talents.[73] Unfortunately, Athenaeus does not say whether it was a gold or a silver talent. At present prices a silver talent (approximate weight given by Webster is fifty-eight pounds) would be valued at $1,900 and a gold talent at $32,000.

Even the youth of Sybaris was expensively clad, for the boys, until they reached the age of manhood, wore purple cloaks (the purple dye was imported from the coasts of Asia Minor and Phoenicia) and had their hair tied in braids which were secured by gold ornaments.[74] The coats worn by the cavalry of Sybaris, which at this time was over five thousand strong, were saffron-colored and were worn over their breastplates.[75] As a contrast to the opulence of the Sybarite, we have an account by Phylarchus, in his twenty-fifth book, of the dress of the Syracusans. He says that among the Syracusans at this time there was a law that a woman should not put on gold ornaments or wear gaily-colored dresses or have garments with purple borders unless she admitted she was a common prostitute. He also says that there was another law that a man might not affect foppish ways or adopt a fancy and conspicuous mode of dress unless he confessed to being an adulterer or a pathic. The free matron was not to go abroad after the sun had set; otherwise it would be a confession that she meant to commit adultery. She was even forbidden to go out by day without the permission of the Supervisors of Women, and then only when accompanied by at least one maid.[76]

It is probably true that many of the accounts of the dissolute life of Sybaris were written with more than a little jealousy by those of their rivals who had not attained to their degree of wealth and luxury, and who, while criticizing their more fortunate neighbors, at the same time endeavored to reach this level of luxury themselves. There are many tales of the laziness and self-indulgence of the true Sybarite. In order to escape the oppressive heat of the valley in summer, they journeyed to the hills and there went to the Grottoes of the Nymphs on the Lusias River and spent their time in every form of luxury.[77] The very name of this summer resort is an indication of the type of life they were leading, and they must have been peculiarly sensitive to the heat unless the climate has changed from that time to this.

When the Sybarite went on a vacation, he traveled in a carriage and always proceeded slowly so that it would take him three days to accomplish an ordinary one-day trip. Furthermore, many of the roads leading to the country are described as having been roofed over.[78] This may very easily refer to the fact that they were lined with trees so that the journey could be made along shaded avenues.

We have already read of their handsomely clad cavalry, and they took great pride in schooling the horses. These were trained to dance to the music of the pipe and were shown as an added attraction at the banqueting hour.[79] The luxury of the training of their horses in this way was to contribute later to the destruction of their city by the Crotoniates. The abundance of slaves also caused them to neglect the development of their own strength and bodies so that they fell easy prey to their opponents in a very brief encounter. This laziness is described in the work of Timaeus, who tells us that a man of Sybaris, going into the country, saw the farmers digging, and told his friends that the sight of such an effort had given him a rupture; one of those who heard him said that listening to him telling such a story had given him a pain in his side.[80] On a visit to the neighboring city of Croton some Sybarites saw an athlete digging up the soil on which the games were to take place. They expressed great surprise that such an important city would not have slaves to dig up the wrestling ground for them.[81] Smindyrides once saw a man digging and swinging his pick and immediately ordered him never to do such a thing in his sight, for it was fatiguing to him to see such effort.[82] Perhaps the final and most extreme example of their luxury and sloth is contained in the story of the patrician who complained of having passed a sleepless night because among the rose leaves on which he slept his slaves had left some crumpled ones.[83]

This wealthy life was provided by the enormous export and import trade carried on by the city. Although the Sybarites dealt with Athens, Corinth, and other cities on the mainland, their principal trade was with Miletus, and the Etruscans.

The site of the port for this trade, Dr. Rainey concluded in 1966, was a settlement of limited size that he found at the long wall. There were no large buildings, but it lay very close to the ancient shore line and probably on the bank of a river, either the Sybaris or the Crati. A possible explanation of this port may be found in the report which Robert L. Raikes, Consulting Engineer, made for the University Museum in 1964. Raikes says, "Round the area where concentrated drilling has taken place there are clear indications of a series of mounds in the sand. These are possibly the remnants of a line of coastal dunes following an earlier shore line, or enclosing a former lagoon." This lagoon might well have provided the harbor which was lacking, the port facilities having been built on the edge of the lagoon.

It is possible that this lagoon provided the harbor for the ships of the Milesians who were the principal source of Eastern trade. Miletus was at the mouth of the Maeander River on the coast of Asia Minor almost directly opposite to Sparta on the mainland. We have told how they had established their own colonies as far as the Black Sea and at the mouth of the Nile. Not only did they supply the Sybarites with dyes and wool, together with luxuries from the East, but the Sybarite felt closer to them culturally than to any other city. We learn from Diodorus[84] that a Sybarite returning home from his travels told his friends that he had seen only one free city, and that was Miletus. When these goods arrived at Sybaris, they were shipped overland across the toe of the Italian boot to the Sybarite cities on the west coast where the ships of the Etruscans would load.

It seems obvious today why this transshipment was the basis for the prosperity of Sybaris. In the first place it was far safer than continuing the voyage by sea, which was subject to great risks from piracy. The Corinthians of Syracuse, in Sicily, were well situated to stop all ships, and the western coasts of Sicily were occupied by the Carthaginians. Were the ships to try to escape both of these marauders and choose to pass through the dangerous strait of Scylla and Charybdis,

I
T
A
L
Y

ETRUSCANS

Tiber River

Rome

ADRIATIC SEA

Naples

Paestum • Metapontum • • Tarentum

Laus • • Sybaris

Cosenza •
• Croton

Messina •
• Rhegium

SICILY

IONIAN SEA

Helice

GREECE

Syracuse •

TYRRHENIAN SEA

MALTA

MEDITERRANEAN SEA

SOUTHERN ITALY

N

MILES

0    50    100    150

River

CA

NIA

thage

C

A

rather than making the long voyage around Sicily, they would be at the mercy of the Chalcidians of Messina.

Comparing this hazardous sea trip of eight days with the overland route which took two or three days, we understand their action. The Sybarites established their ports on the west coast; Laus, which was probably the most important but has never been found; Skidros; Sirinus; and Paestum (Poseidonia), whose extent and beauty are apparent to us today.

For many generations the Chalcidians from Greece had a monopoly on the trade between the Aegean and the west coast of Italy and southern France. Their colony at Cumae above Naples was the northernmost outpost of the Greeks. The Sybarites were not long in grasping the strategic advantage of their location on the southern shore of the narrow peninsula. By building their own colonies, they were able to thwart the navies of the Chalcidians, Corinthians, or Carthaginians. Unloading their imports at Sybaris, and being able to see the Tyrrhenian Sea from the mountains nearby, they could easily transport these goods over the mountains with animals and deliver them to the waiting Etruscan ships on the west coast. What they did might be compared to the voyage through the Suez Canal in preference to the long and hazardous trip around the Cape of Good Hope. The naval defeat of the Etruscans in the fifth century, however, probably put an end to this traffic and furthered the decline of these colonies, the mother city of Sybaris having already been demolished.

# VIII

# COLONIES OF SYBARIS

One of the impelling reasons for the search for Sybaris was what we can see at Paestum, the ancient Poseidonia, and this is only one of four similar cities which the Sybarites built. Paestum was originally built near the sea, about the end of the seventh century,[85] but it was later moved inland and surrounded with the walls which we see today. The question naturally arose whether the Sybarites did the same, and if they built near the sea should we not find early buildings there? Up until recently, the buildings found on the coast were almost all later than Sybaris. Paestum provides us with a map of what we are looking for and, until we have unearthed Sybaris, there is no better example that can be described. One day spent at Paestum will explain the burning desire of the archaeologist to excavate the city which gave birth to such unique buildings and to try to uncover what may remain of the superb temples of Sybaris. They must have been no less beautiful than what we can see at Paestum and may even have surpassed them.

The walls of Paestum were about three miles in circumference and of irregular shape, and the city was crossed by two main roads entering through gates at the four points of the compass. The city is built on a flat plain and, unlike Athens or Agrigentum, there is no acropolis crowned by temples. Today's walls have been rebuilt by both the Lucanians and the Romans and in some places are over twenty feet thick. There are many small gates reinforced by towers, as well as the four main gates. Around the city is a moat, and two of the bridges over the moat are still partially preserved. Some of the walls may still be identified as belonging to the time of Sybaris.

On entering the main gate, one is opposite the Temple of Neptune. On the left is the Basilica and on the right the Temple of Ceres. This part of the city was known as the Sacred Area, and Virgil sang of the roses which bloomed there in spring and fall,[86] which they still do today. The Basilica was built in the middle of the sixth century, or a hundred years before the Parthenon in Athens, and is about 170 by 80 feet. Almost one hundred years later these settlers from Sybaris, after the downfall of the mother city, built the Temple of Neptune, of imposing proportions and perhaps the finest existing Doric temple. It is approximately eighty feet wide and two hundred in length. To an architect, the columns of this temple, seven feet in diameter at the base, tapering to five at the top, provide a fascinating study. The columns at the ends of the temple are slightly smaller than the ones on the sides, and at the corners the columns are elliptical and not circular. By this extraordinarily carefully thought out plan, the view of the temple from any angle gives a beautifully harmonious appearance. The Greeks would never have been satisfied with the modern uniform and box-like methods of today's architects. The smallest temple, that

*Temple of Neptune, Paestum*

of Ceres, is also Doric and was built about the year 520. Throughout this area of the city are the ruins of other small temples and altars of later dates.

About the year 400 the city was overcome by the Lucanians, who held it for over one hundred years, until they were finally conquered by the Romans in A.D. 273, and it was at this time that it was given its modern name. The city remained faithful to the Romans during the Punic Wars, furnishing them with gold from its temples and sending ships loaded with grain to the relief of Tarentum when it was besieged by Hannibal. The Saracens sacked and partly destroyed Paestum in A.D. 871, and the city, now deserted, sank back into the malarial marshes. It was not until the middle of the eighteenth century that it was rediscovered, when a road was being built through it.

Paestum prospered greatly not only from the rich farm land surrounding it, but also from the trade with the Etruscans who came there to exchange their goods for the merchandise which the Sybarites had sent across the mountains.

The territory of the Etruscans covered the western side of the Apennines from Pisa to Rome, and was a rich and highly developed country in agriculture, wines, and manufactures. Strangely enough, the cultivated olive, which now covers the hillsides of Italy, apparently was unknown there in early times,[87] and they were importing their oil from Attica. The Etruscans were able to supply the Greeks with iron, tin, copper, axes, and farming implements, and, if needed, with grain and timber. They were also proficient in the weaving of flax for sails. The Etruscans developed a famous navy which ruled the Tyrrhenian Sea until its final defeat by Hiero I of Syracuse in 474. However, their principal trade with the Greeks was most probably in their metals, particularly since iron was replacing bronze and was of the greatest importance for the use of troops.

That the Etruscans led a life of ease and opulence is told in accounts by the ancient authors. Diodorus[88] says that "the land the Tyrrhenians inhabit bears every crop, and from the intensive cultivation of it they enjoy no lack of fruits, not only sufficient for their sustenance but contributing to abundant enjoyment and luxury.

"For example, twice each day they spread costly tables and upon them everything that is appropriate to excessive luxury, providing gay coloured couches and having ready at hand a multitude of silver drinking-cups of every description and servants-in-waiting in no small numbers; and these attendants are some of them of exceeding comeliness and others

are arrayed in clothing more costly than befits the station of a
slave . . . and passing their lives as they do in drinking-bouts
and unmanly amusements, it is easily understood how they
have lost the glory of warfare which their fathers possessed.
Not the least of the things which have contributed to their
luxury is the fertility of the land; for since it bears every
product of the soil and is altogether fertile, the Tyrrhenians
lay up great stores of every kind of fruit."

Theopompus, who was apparently a notorious gossip, is
quoted by Athenaeus[89] in the following passage to show the
decadence of these people:

"Among the Etruscans, who had become extravagantly
luxurious Timaeus records in his first book that the slave girls
wait on men naked. And Theopompus in the forty-third
book of his Histories says that it is customary with the
Etruscans to share their women in common; the women
bestow great care on their bodies and often exercise even
with men, sometimes also with one another; for it is no disgrace for women to show themselves naked. Further, they
dine, not with their own husbands, but with any men who
happen to be present, and they pledge with wine any whom
they wish. They are also terribly bibulous, and are very
good-looking. The Etruscans rear all the babies that are born,
not knowing who the father is in any single case. These in
turn pursue the same mode of life as those who have given
them nurture, having drinking parties often and consorting
with all the women. It is no disgrace for Etruscans to be seen
doing anything in the open, or even having anything done
to them; for this also is a custom of their country. And so far
are they from regarding it as a disgrace that they actually say,
when the master of the house is indulging in a love affair,
and someone inquires for him, that he is undergoing so and
so, openly calling the act by its indecent name. When they

get together for companionship or in family parties they do
as follows: first of all, after they have stopped drinking and
are ready to go to bed, the servants bring in to them, the
lamps being still lighted, sometimes female prostitutes, sometimes very beautiful boys, sometimes also their wives; and
when they have enjoyed these, the servants then introduce
lusty young men, who in their turn consort with them. They
indulge in love affairs and carry on these unions sometimes
in full view of one another, but in most cases with screens set
up around the beds; the screens are made of latticed wands,
over which cloths are thrown. Now they consort very eagerly,
to be sure, with women; much more, however, do they enjoy
consorting with boys and striplings."

In addition to the fertility of their land and their vast
forests they were rich in sources of metal which they used not
only at home, but also in the export trade, by which they
gained great wealth and which they carried on not only with
the Sybarites, but with other peoples as well. An accurate
account of this is available to us in Diodorus:[90]

"Off the city of Tyrrhenia known as Poplonium there is
an island which men called Aethaleia [Elba]. It is about one
hundred stades distance from the coast and received the name
it bears from the smoke which lies so thick about it. For the
island possesses a great amount of iron rock, and they possess
a great abundance of this ore. For those who are engaged in
the working of the ore crush the rock and burn the lumps
which have thus been broken in certain ingenious furnaces;
and in these they smelt the lumps by means of a great fire
and form them into pieces of moderate size which are in
their appearance like large sponges. These are purchased by
merchants in exchange either for money or for goods and
are then taken to Dicaearcheia [Puteoli] or the other trading
stations, where there are men who purchase such cargoes and

who, with the aid of a multitude of artisans in metal whom
they have collected, work it further and manufacture iron
objects, of every description. Some of these are worked into
the shape of armor, and others are ingeniously fabricated into
shapes well suited for two-pronged forks and sickles and other
such tools; and these are then carried by merchants to every
region and thus many parts of the inhabited world have a
share in the usefulness which accrues from them."

The account of these mines is confirmed by both Virgil
and Strabo.[91] In spite, or perhaps because, of their great
wealth the Etruscans had a streak of cruelty in their nature,
and Virgil,[92] in speaking of Mezentius, their king, says,

> "Why tell of unspeakable murder and deed
> In human? The Gods on the tyrant requite them,
>     and on his seed!
> Nay, he would knit to the living the dead,
>     shackle limb unto limb
> And face unto face—that cunning device
>     of torments grim!
> And so by a lingering death the life
>     from his victims he tore
> Locked in that awful embrace with
>     the slime of corruption and gore."

This was the race which, together with the Milesians in
Asia Minor, were the principal customers of Sybaris, and the
Sybarites felt a closer tie to their way of living than with that
of any other peoples.

To return to the cities established by the Sybarites on
the west coast of Italy, perhaps the most important of these
from a trading standpoint was Laus, as it was the point on
that coast most easily reached from Sybaris. Both it and
Paestum issued their own coins, but it may be that this did
not occur until after the fall of the mother city when some

of its inhabitants took up their residence in Laus.[93] This city lay in a small plain on the west coast at the mouth of the river Lao, and it was probably to this port or possibly Skidros that the Etruscan ships first came to deliver their goods to the Sybarites, who in turn had brought the wool, pottery, and other goods from Asia from the east coast across the mountains. Dunbabin, the modern authority on Magna Graecia, has given us an excellent description of the route which could have been taken, and in fact he followed this route and two others through the passes in severe weather, including snowstorms. He tells us that the distance is approximately forty miles and that the trip could have been made in two days on foot with pack animals. This intervening territory was not all settled by the Greeks, but it seems probable that the natives were either subject to, or controlled by, the Sybarites. The ease, speed, and safety of this route over the dangers from piracy, the length, and hazards of the sea trip are readily apparent, and the route must have been open except in the depths of winter when the snow lay too heavily.

In thinking of the Greek city-states of this period and in speaking of the citizens, it is well to bear in mind that each citizen had his slaves, which might vary from one to over a thousand; so that when the population of a city was given, the actual number of citizens might not be more than a tenth of the total number of people living there. Also, the figures for the population might refer not only to the city itself, but also to the other cities and tribes which were ruled over by the mother city. This is undoubtedly the case with Sybaris when we read the large figures used by the ancient authors. As I have said, the "polis" was a community and was ruled as a whole with the government being the concern of all its citizens. In Sophocles's *Antigone*,[94] Haemon says, "A polis for one man is no polis at all." We are not told the exact form of oligarchy, but it is probable that Sybaris was ruled either by certain chosen citizens or by a few noble families. In either case the choice of these rulers was made by their fellow citizens, and it is almost certain that this ruling class was also made up of those who were the wealthiest. Usually the polis was small enough and the people sufficiently cohesive that the whole body of citizens could be heard on matters affecting their government.

In the decisions made by the ancient Greek cities the gods and the oracles were frequently consulted. Imagination and apprehension played a considerable part in all their affairs, and long voyages would be made to consult the oracle before embarking on some enterprise. The Sybarites once sent men, one of whom was Amyris, to consult the oracle in Greece because they wanted to learn how long they would enjoy prosperity. The oracles always seem to have played their game on the safe side, for their answers were often ambiguous and could be interpreted both ways. Unfortunately, the suppliant usually understood it in the way most favorable to him. In this case the Pythian priestess replied: "Happy, thou Sybarite, all happy shalt thou ever be in thy abundance, whilst honoring the race of them that live forever." This sounds like a good guarantee that, as long as they brought gifts to the gods, they would continue in luxury. She went on to say, "But whensoever thou hold a mortal man in awe rather than a god, then shall war and civil strife come upon thee."[95] They interpreted this to mean that they would never stop living their life of ease and abundance, for they could not imagine that they would ever honor a human being more than a god. They did not have long to wait, and the change in their fortunes came about when a man was flogging one of his slaves and continued beating him after he had fled to the sanctuaries; but when, finally, the slave ran to the tomb of his masters' father, the master let him go out of reverence for his father. This was thought to be a direct disobedience

of the gods, for the master had shown more honor to the
tomb and memory of his father than he had to the sanctuaries
of the gods, and we are told that, not long after this, Sybaris
was destroyed.[96] The government of local affairs was a constant source of interest to the public, and the decisions taken
were frequently based on signs and auguries from the gods,
which they would often talk about in the barbershop. Barbers
seem to have been as voluble and as confident in their opinion
of the best way to run the state in those days as they are now.

In the matter of the Olympic games they also tempted
the gods. The city fathers of Sybaris, anticipating by twenty-
five hundred years the action of their present-day counterparts
in their overpowering desire to be a World's Fair city, decided to set up rival games. Scymnus[97] writes that it is said
they ceased following the laws of Zaleucus and chose instead
to lead a life of luxury and laziness; after a time they degen-
erated so far that they attempted to bring an end to the
Olympic games and destroy the honors due to Zeus. This they
attempted by the following plan: At great expense (memories
of the New York World's Fair 1964–65) they held a gym-
nastic contest in honor of Zeus at the same time as the
Eleians, who held the Olympic games, so that men, attracted
by the prospect of reward, might desert Greece and come to
Sybaris.[98] Soon afterward the city of Sybaris fell in battle and
was destroyed.[99] They had never been famous for their athletes and, in distinction from other Greek cities, there is only
one mention of success on their part, which was at the forty-
first festival of the Olympics when boxing for boys was introduced and the winner from those who entered this event for
the first time was Philytas of Sybaris.[100] A few miles from
Sybaris archaeologist Dottoressa Paola Zancani Montuoro has
unearthed a contemporary tablet recording a dedication to
Athena in thanks for a victory at Olympia.

# IX

# CROTON

In the year 510 the incredible happened. Sybaris, the envy of all, its inhabitants leading a life of ease and luxury, in a few short weeks was a pile of smoking ruins heaped with the dead bodies of her men. Furthermore, this destruction was accomplished by a city of fellow Achaeans who had no desire for war.

The destroyer of Sybaris was Croton, founded a few years after Sybaris on the coast seventy-five miles to the west. On this beautiful shore of the Ionian Sea, the only harbor except distant Tarentum was chosen in the hope that ships would find it a profitable trading port. The founder of Croton was Myscellus of Rhypes,[101] who first visited Sybaris. He was so impressed by what he saw that he returned to Greece to consult the gods, as he did not feel it was possible to develop a rival city. He was told to return to the harbor site and build.[102]

Although the harbor was an advantage, Croton never attained the riches of Sybaris. This was for two reasons: There was only a small amount of fertile land between the coast and the mountains, and the mountains at this point had no easy passage for the Crotoniates to reach the western coast of Italy for trading with the Etruscans. The rigorous life which they led was in strong contrast to the dissolute ways of Sybaris. The Crotoniates admired physical fitness and spent much time in training, so that their men became hardy and valorous soldiers. They were famous at Olympia, and Milo of Croton was the greatest athlete of the age, being the victor six times at the Olympic games. A man of superb physique, he was accustomed to wear his Olympic crown and only a lion skin when he went into battle, thus aping Hercules.[103] We have seen that there is no record of a cultural or intellectual life at Sybaris. Quite the contrary is true of Croton. It became famous as having the greatest school of medicine in Magna Graecia, and scholars from far-off Greece came to sit at the feet of Pythagoras to learn from his mathematical genius and to join in his philosophical discussions.

Pythagoras came to Croton in 529 from his native island of Samos. Founding a school, he rapidly became the leader of the learned life of the city. He taught the equality of the sexes some 150 years before Plato. Dividing his talents between philosophy, astronomy, and mathematics, he developed the theory of transmigration, and in mathematics he is credited with many discoveries.

In the year 510 the wealth and arrogance of the oligarchy then ruling Sybaris aroused the mass of the citizens, and various charges were brought against the most influential leaders by a citizen named Telys.[104] By his arguments he persuaded the tribunal to exile five hundred of the richest men and to confiscate all their property. This act led to the downfall of the city. The five hundred took refuge at the altar in the market place of Croton, causing Telys to send ambassadors to demand their immediate return and to threaten war. Since

Sybaris was far larger, richer, and more powerful than Croton, this presented the grave problem of the possible destruction of Croton and the massacre of its population. At the meeting held to consider this threat, the sentiment of the Crotoniates was to accede to the demand and deliver up all those who had come to them for protection. At this point Pythagoras addressed the assembly, urging his fellow citizens not to disgrace the good name of their city by relinquishing their unwanted guests. His argument prevailed, and thirty ambassadors were sent to Sybaris to arrive at an amicable agreement.[105]

These thirty men were the leaders of Croton, although Pythagoras fortunately was not among them. On their arrival at Sybaris, Telys ordered them all murdered. Their bodies were thrown over the walls of the city to be eaten by the wolves.[106] (We have in this statement a direct reference to Sybaris as a walled city.) This treacherous act had immediate and violent repercussions. The gods showed their anger with the Sybarites, and the statue of Hera, the wife of Zeus, poured forth blood. The flow was so great that they were forced to close the bronze doors of the temple to prevent its rising in the city.[107] The mob now took matters into its own hands, overthrew the temporary rulers, and killed Telys and all his followers on the steps of the altar, thus again incurring the wrath of the gods for the desecration of the altar.[108]

War was now inevitable. The murder of ambassadors was an unheard-of offense which caused the immediate mobilizing of the armies. Diodorus tells us that Croton prepared to attack with a force of 100,000 under the leadership of Milo and that opposed to them was an army of 300,000 Sybarites.[109] These figures seem to be wildly exaggerated when we realize the population of the cities. The armies met on the plain, and in the first encounter the rout of the Sybarites was complete. The strategy of the Crotoniates had probably never been used before, nor has it been used again. Being familiar with the tunes which the horses danced to on festive occasions, they trained pipers to play this music. In a fragment of Aristotle there is an account of a flute player of the Sybarites who, in revenge for an insult, revealed this dance tune to the Crotoniates. When they began their advance and were within bowshot range of the gleaming armor of the Sybarite cavalry, the Croton pipers struck up the dance tune. The well-trained horses immediately began to dance, and their riders were unable to control them in order to charge. This not only threw the cavalry into confusion but made them dance into the lines of their infantry, causing complete demoralization. The Sybarites literally danced to defeat.[110] Following this catastrophe, the Sybarites withdrew within the walls of their city. After a siege of seventy days the Crotoniates entered the city, and a scene of carnage ensued. No prisoners were taken, and all who were unable to escape were killed on the spot, the city being turned over to the troops for looting and destruction. The wealth of the Sybarites was carried off to Croton, and the city itself was laid waste.[111] After the pillage of Sybaris and its probable burning, the Crotoniates "conducted the river over it and submerged it."[112]

These statements are extremely important to the archaeologist, for if the city was plundered, to what extent was this done? Did they remove the statuary and larger works of art, or did they simply topple them from their bases and leave them in situ? How much time and effort did they use to tear down the temples? Did they simply burn them and leave the columns and walls standing? That there could have been a fire is indicated by the number of blackened roof tiles of this period which we found in the summer of 1964. In any case, it is hard to believe that they would have bothered to carry out complete devastation if they were to divert the river over the city. The quotation of Strabo on the diverting of the river is the only mention of this flooding, and he was writing some five hundred years after the event. This was also a frequent explanation given for the loss of some historic monument, as in the sixth century of the Christian era we have already read how Jordanes described the building of the tomb of the Visigothic king, Alaric, in the bed of the Busento River, the river being returned to its former bed to hide the still undiscovered site of the tomb. If the river at Sybaris was diverted, how far inland was this diversion made? Does it mean that this is the reason why the present-day Coscile River joins the Crati, when in olden times they had separate mouths to the sea?

We have read that the Sybarites had not developed any military leaders. In this battle they called on a famous foreign general, Hieron, to be their commander. A man without principles, he put his brother in command of the vanguard in the hope that he would be killed.[113] The Sybarites claimed that the Crotoniates also needed outside leadership and had brought in Dorieus as their general. This was denied by Croton, which claimed that the only help they had was from Callias, an Elean Diviner.[114] To prove that Croton needed outside help, the Sybarites later showed a precinct and a temple beside the dry bed of the Crati which Dorieus founded in honor of Athena for the help he received in taking the city. This account is given by Herodotus, who was writing at the neighboring city of Thurii in 439.[115] If this temple was apparently still standing on the shore of the Crati after the destruction of the city, where is it today? Does it lie beneath the enormous deposit of soil which has been washed down from the mountains over the centuries? Was it destroyed by an earthquake or soil subsidence? It is also of especial interest because the account was written only seventy years after the fall of Sybaris and could easily mean that in Herodotus we have an eyewitness to the existence of a great temple at Sybaris.

Herodotus died and was buried at Thurii, and his ashes, according to Stephanus Byzantius,[116] lie in this plain of his adopted city, to which he fled after escaping from his fatherland when his kinsman was executed for treason.

The ruins of Sybaris lay unoccupied for fifty-eight years, but in the year 452 an attempt was made to resettle the city. A Thessalian gathered together a group of former inhabitants and took them back to Sybaris. The account would imply that it was in the same location and definitely states that it was between the Sybaris and the Crati Rivers. They were able to till the same fertile soil, and they quickly regained some of the wealth which they had lost. However, they had been there only a few years when their "jealous and more powerful neighbors again drove them out."[117]

This raises a very important question for those seeking Sybaris. If the city was totally destroyed and if the river was diverted over it, had the river again changed its course, and why would they have resettled a destroyed city? It would seem that it would have been far easier to build another city adjacent to the old one. It also leads us to think that the original destruction of the city may not have been so complete as described; otherwise, why would they have resettled? There still may be great ruined buildings, statuary, and pottery in Sybaris.

There was ample land, and certainly history has given us innumerable instances of the use of older buildings as a source of material for new ones. Perhaps the Coliseum in Rome is as good an example as any, for it was used as a quarry for many years and some of the great palaces of Rome were embellished with its marble. The cutting of the enormous blocks of stone must have consumed endless hours, as they were all cut with such accuracy that they fitted together without the use of any binding material. The wall unearthed by the University Museum shows the size of these blocks, as can readily be seen in the illustration on page 147. The indication is that there were buildings and streets still in the old city after fifty years and that this may have been the site of the refounding of the city, but nothing of this is known definitely.

With the driving out of the Sybarites for the second time, we come to the final end of the city, and there is no further mention of any later events there in early historical accounts, except by reference to its former glory.

# X

# PRIOR EXPEDITIONS

The earliest report of the many archaeologists who have sought Sybaris was made in 1879 by the famous Italian Cavallari. At this time the plain was not drained or inhabited because of the prevalence of malaria, which some believe may have caused the abandonment of cultivation as far back as the tenth century A.D.

Francesco Cavallari, Director of the Museum at Syracuse, Sicily, was assigned by the Italian Ministry of Public Instruction to make investigations at Sybaris. He began his work in the foothills above the plain and on the north bank of the Crati River. On the west of the hill called Apollinara, not far from the juncture of the two rivers, he found quantities of sherds, a terracotta figurine, a coin, a terracotta head, and a clay vessel, and he noted that these were archaic and could have been from ancient Sybaris. The term "archaic" applies to work done prior to the sixth century. Hellenic work was between the sixth and fourth centuries, and Hellenistic followed the Hellenic (these are rough dates). Downstream on

the south bank of the Crati and east of the Fonte del Fico he
found a Hellenistic necropolis which might have been associated with Thurii. He also excavated a group of conical mounds
where he found a tomb containing human bones, bronze
handles, a silver breast plaque with a female head in relief,
hairpins, and two golden strips with Greek inscriptions of
prayers. Cavallari was emphatic that no pottery which could
be dated earlier than the fifth century was found in these
tombs and, therefore, none could have been from Sybaris.
Realizing that the water brought to him by the peasants came
from the spring of Fonte del Fico, he accepted it as being the
famous one of Thurii and found the start of the aqueduct.
Cavallari also noted two groups of ruined buildings of brick
and tile construction in the area of the spring. He believed
the most likely site for Sybaris was in the region between the
Crati and the Coscile, just above their present junction.

François Lenormant, Professor of Archaeology at the
Bibliothèque Nationale in Paris, visited Sybaris at about the
same time as Cavallari and wrote his work, *La Grande Grèce*,
in 1880. It is very complete for the entire area of Magna
Graecia and makes quite fascinating reading. Unfortunately,
there are no notes in the book and he does not provide the
reader with references as to his sources of knowledge. I made
inquiries at both the Bibliothèque Nationale and at the
Sorbonne when I was in Paris, but I was unable to find any
documents which show where he obtained his information.
Under the circumstances I think that what he tells us will
have to be questioned unless later information will show his
sources. He tells us that only Cumae and Locri were founded
before Sybaris, and that the colonists used the type of writing
which was peculiar to Achaea, and the Dorian dialect which
was used in their homeland. One of his most interesting
statements is that a system of well-conceived canals drained

the low parts of the plain and that these canals were navigable, being used by the Sybarites to transport the wine from the hills either to the city or to the ships of the foreign traders which were in the port awaiting them. I have found no mention of canals in the writings of over eighty ancient Greek and Roman authors.

He also speaks of silver mines in the valley of the Trionto and states that these were still in use in the year A.D. 1558, until the influx of this metal from Central America caused the closing of the mines. He writes that there were silver mines also at Argentanum in the valley of the Crati in Roman times. He cites these silver properties as the reason for the large number of coins of Sybaris, but as I have found no mention of silver mining in the ancient authors I assume the prevalence of Sybaris coins to be due to the size of the city and the foreign trade it carried on with the Etruscans, the Greeks of Asia Minor, and the homeland. He further tells us that between the mouths of the two rivers there was a small bay formed by the deposit of the alluvial soil at the shore line, that he could still see the ancient outline of this bay, and that the ancient authors praised the security of this small basin. It is possible that Lenormant saw the remains of the lagoon described by Raikes, but there is no reference by ancient authors praising a bay, and again Lenormant gives no source for his statement.

Lenormant also states that when the Crotoniates defeated the Sybarites and took the city, they proceeded methodically to destroy its ramparts and tear down all the important buildings and, with all the most solemn religious rites, he avers that they pronounced terrible imprecations, calling down the wrath of the gods on whoever would dare to attempt to raise Sybaris from its ruins. Again no reference to which author.

These statements of Lenormant would be of great in-

terest to those looking for Sybaris if we knew from what
sources he had drawn his information. If the Sybarites had
navigable canals, it could very well mean that the city lay
inland and not on the sea, whereas the ruins which have been
shown by the instruments all lie near the coast. On the other
hand, if we had any early references to a basin or harbor near
the city, these would be a clear indication that the Museum
would have been correct in looking for the city at a point
where the rivers in ancient times were close to one another
as they entered the sea. Lenormant wrote that the Crotoniates
tore down the walls and the principal buildings. It is hard to
understand why they would have undertaken such an enormous
task if they were then going to bury the city beneath the
waters of a river. At the height of its power the walls of
Sybaris, as described by Strabo, were over five miles in circumference and, judging by the walls of Paestum, which the
Sybarites built, and which may still be measured today from
fifteen to twenty feet thick, the destruction of the walls of
Sybaris would have been an enormous as well as a seemingly
unnecessary task. Also we know of many instances where
older buildings with their huge blocks of stone, already shaped
and fitted, have been used in the construction of new buildings, and the Crotoniates would have deprived themselves
of this vast, ready-made quarry if they had diverted the river
over the ruins as well.

Lenormant goes on to say that six kilometers from the
bridge of the river Crati he examined a plateau which is raised
in a small promontory in a bend of the river, and on this hill
were found the ruins of ancient buildings, in sufficient number to indicate clearly that it had been the site of a city which
had been destroyed. The same ruins were found on the opposite side of the valley where the torrent of Mosolito enters
the Crati River.

He states definitely that these ruins are those of Thurii—

or more exactly of the Roman city of Copiae on the site of Thurii—and that to find the ruins of Thurii proper it is necessary only to excavate at this point. He says that the plan of the city as described by the ancient authors as being in the form of a rectangle was perfectly clear to him on the site. Lenormant gives the site of the city as running in a northeast and southeast direction for about two and one half kilometers, and in the opposite direction for about one kilometer. The agora, he says, was in the valley of the Mosolito, between the two hills a short distance from the spring of Thurii, which is now called the Fonte del Fico. He also tells of the multiplicity of ruins on the plateau of Le Muraglie.

In speaking of his search for Sybaris, Lenormant believed that there were definite indications by which the site could be determined with mathematical certainty and says that his exploration conforms absolutely with the studies made by Cavallari, and that Sybaris could only possibly be located at this one point. He states that in 510 B.C. the Crotoniates must have deflected the Crati River at the northern point of Le Muraglie in order to have the river wind back and forward over the ruins of Sybaris. This was very clear to him from where he stood, and he is definite that the ruins of the city must be sought where the Crati leaves its ancient bed. He gives various other facts about this site, even to mentioning a chapel which the Sybarites must have constructed, and he concludes that the city must be in this area and can be nowhere else. He also mentions that the city must be fifteen to twenty feet below the present level and that it will be necessary to pump out the water, which begins about six feet down. In this he was correct.

In writing of his discoveries, Lenormant ends with a fervent plea to the French Government in these words:

"But also what marvelous results await those who will

have the courage to undertake this Herculean task! No matter what amounts may be spent one can be sure that they will not be regretted. One speaks a great deal of science at this time [1880] and certainly the authorities display the most praiseworthy liberality to serve its interest and to contribute to its progress. But here [in France] in official circles they are too disposed to only support chemistry, astronomy or natural history. Far be it from me to plead that they do too much for them. However, it is time to be inspired somewhat by the example given to our Assembly by the House of Commons of England and the Reichstag of Berlin, in the large subsidies that they have freely given to the excavations of Halicarnassus, Ephesus, Olympia and Pergamum. The exhumation of great works of antique art is no lesser a service rendered to civilization than the discovery of a new chemical formula. They understand this in foreign countries; it was formerly understood in our country, but now too long a time has passed and France has ceased to hold a rank worthy of her in great archaeological explorations and monumental excavations, where she reaped so much glory with the Egyptian expedition, the Commission of Morée, the works of Champollion and of Botta, and where today her rivals reap the honors. One must make an effort to raise the level of classical studies, to restore to them the life which they have lost. The first and surest way to restore them to the public taste is to involve the national honor in these enterprises, which serve art and learning so powerfully and which reveal from their tomb the splendors of the past. But it is important to make haste if we wish to decide to renew the continuity of one of the most brilliant traditions of our country, in rivalling the example of the English and the Germans. The number of places in the classical world where the ruins can prove really fruitful is not unlimited. There are hardly five or six untouched places where exploration appears the most productive, but which cannot remain intact for long. Let us hope the day does not come when the Government of France will repent too late of its long indifference, by seeing that it has let pass, what cannot be retrieved, the opportunity of adding a new jewel in the crown of our country.

"Of all places where archaeological exploration remains to be done, that place where it will give surest and greatest results, I do not hesitate to say, is Sybaris. The destruction of this city was so sudden that it may be compared to those cities engulfed by Vesuvius in its eruption in the year 79 A.D. The hatred of the Crotoniates overthrew the buildings of the proscribed city, but even this destruction has put the debris under protection from the ordinary ravages of time. The precaution taken by the destroyers to make the ruins disappear in a few years, under the soil carried by the river, has also provided a conservation similar to the rain of cinders from the volcano of Campania. They have escaped the slow dissolution which awaits all ruins that can be exploited as a quarry. It is a veritable Pompeii of the eighth to the sixth century before the Christian era, which is buried under the waters of the slowly winding Crati. It is even too little to say a Pompeii, because it is not just a small city of the third or fourth order, but indeed the largest and richest city of the period. An entire civilization, still only imperfectly known, will emerge from these ruins. It will be a veritable resurrection, which will take place at the moment when it had attained its highest degree of development, and without any mixture of later ages. The soil of Sybaris, from the spade of the excavators, will reveal the complete picture of the Greek culture in the centuries when it began to have its own consciousness and to assume its own physiognomy. Could there be anything more interesting for history?

"We consider that the temples of Poseidonia-Paestum are one of the most justly admired types of Greek architecture in all that is virile and most grandiose. Since these temples are only those of a secondary city, a colony of Sybaris, and the most beautiful of all was built at a time when Paestum was a dependency and had to obtain its artists from Sybaris— what then may have been those of the metropolis? There are certainly, under the layers of alluvial soil which cover Sybaris, temples as gigantic as that of Selinunte, with its sculptures of the same period, and perhaps even more interesting, which lie overturned, but without any debris which can detract from them. This is what excavations on a grand scale in the valley of the Crati will restore to the light of day, which will repay the efforts and expense of those who undertake them. The obstacles to overcome are great, but they are not insurmountable."

After Lenormant, the next important search was done in 1887–88 by Professor Luigi Viola, Director of the Museum at Taranto. His work had a striking similarity to that of the University Museum almost eighty years later. He began in the area mentioned by Cavallari and Lenormant at the junction of the two rivers, and speaks of waiting for the "long and patient work of the drills," just as we have waited today. While waiting, he moved some seven miles farther inland to the foothills, and there he worked at Torre del Mordillo and excavated between the Esaro and Coscile Rivers. He found nothing with his drills, but in March, 1888, he excavated on Torre del Mordillo and listed the contents of over two hundred tombs, which were extremely interesting. He and Luigi Pigorino concluded that the material found in the tombs could be dated between 720 and 520, but that they were not Greek, and he defined them simply as "Italic." There were skeletons, bronze razors, swords, iron axes, and pottery.

What is most curious about his discoveries is that what he found was totally different from the objects which were found on Torre del Mordillo in 1963 and 1967 by the University Museum and which will be explained later.

No further work by eminent archaeologists was done until 1928–30, when Professor Edoardo Galli, superintendent of Antiquities of Calabria, began excavating about five miles farther inland from the joining of the two streams at a site called Grotta del Malconsiglio on the south bank of the Coscile River. Here was found a building which was probably a Roman farm, containing a large number of rooms and storage vats; one large underground room of the Roman Imperial period is still intact. Nearby are some fine mosaic pavements and stuccoed and painted walls, one room having columns and open at the top. The most interesting part of Galli's discoveries was large blocks of tufa in the foundation of the building. They showed excellent workmanship and much weathering before their use in this building. He concluded from the quantity and the size of these blocks in the foundation that they suggest a vast ruin of the Greek age somewhere in the immediate neighborhood. Perhaps from the ruins of Sybaris? He also found some fine Hellenistic pottery, terracotta masks, and an archaic marble head.

At the time Galli was there, the Government was engaged in an extensive project of restoring the plain to its original use as a great agricultural area. They were excavating canals, drilling wells, building new roads, and two new villages, bridging the rivers, and channeling them and the *torrenti* with embankments. (A *torrente* is a huge river bed, the melting snow from the mountains flooding it in the spring, but completely dry the rest of the year. Before the *torrenti* were confined, for centuries they flooded the entire plain.) All of this was of interest to the archaeologist as to what might be unearthed or found in the drilling of the wells. A few tombs only were found in the course of this vast work, and even with the deep piers sunk for the bridges no ruins were struck. Many of the holes went below fifteen feet in the construction of the villages, but nothing was found. The wells were drilled in some places to a depth of over two hundred feet with no trace of sherds or masonry.

Galli's conclusions were that there were a port, sanctuaries and estates on the hills, and a necropolis.

Professor Ulrich Kahrstedt, of the University of Göttingen, wrote two articles on his trip to Magna Graecia in 1931, and concluded that the Coscile River is not the ancient Sybaris River, but that the present-day San Mauro probably is, and therefore that Sybaris should be found south of the Crati.

Senator Umberto Zanotti-Bianco, in 1932, excavated in this area to prove Kahrstedt's theory. He dug in the *timparelli* or mounds which Kahrstedt believed to be the ancient necropolis of Sybaris and found nothing but sand dunes. He also opened a series of trenches in this area, but went to a depth of only seven feet. From this he concluded that there was no basis for Kahrstedt's theory, although today we would feel that these excavations were far too shallow to show any results. He then moved north of the Crati and quickly found a large Roman building in the Parco del Cavallo area. In addition to various pieces of glass and pottery of Roman origin, he found an archaic head of the time of Sybaris. His final conclusion was that Sybaris would be found not far from the sea in what was then a low malarial area.

Dottoressa Paola Zancani Montuoro, a brilliant Italian archaeologist famous for her work at Paestum and the Sele, Francavilla, and other sites, describes the collections from the 1932 excavations and concludes that some of the architectural fragments are from a small archaic temple and could not have been brought there either by man or by any natural phenomena. She also includes a map of 1602 showing the Coscile and Crati entering the sea from separate mouths.

Donald Freeman Brown, of the Peabody Museum of Harvard University and a Fellow of the American Academy in Rome, worked in the plain from 1949 to 1953, and his conclusion was that Sybaris lay on both sides of the Crati River two miles from its mouth. He devised a drill which enabled him to bring up a complete column of earth from the subsoil. These samples led him to conclude that he had defined an area which had been occupied for the last six centuries before Christ, with three levels of occupation; an upper Roman, a fourth-century Greek, and a sixth-century Greek.

In trying to pinpoint the location of Sybaris from a study of the work done by these eminent archaeologists, it can be seen quickly that we do not have any uniform consensus as to the exact site. We have both Cavallari and Lenormant believing that the city lay to the west of the present juncture of the Coscile and the Crati and running back to the foothills of Apollinara and Le Muraglie, and Lenormant was quite positive in his views. Galli also located the city in this general area, but Kahrstedt believed the city lay to the south of the Crati and between it and the San Mauro, whereas Zanotti-Bianco placed it near the sea, and Brown concluded that it lay on both sides of the Crati.

From the work of these archaeologists we could deduce only that the city might lie in an area of almost twenty square miles bounded by the sea on the east, the hill of Apollinara on the west, the San Mauro River on the south, and the Coscile River on the north. Also it might be twenty or more feet below the present surface. However, we had the writings of the ancient authors saying that it lay in a hollow between two rivers and that the sea stretched beside it. A formidable task still lay ahead of us in this large area.

# XI

# THE SEARCH

I n writing of the work at Sybaris, I shall frequently use
the term "we," but when I say "we" I mean the University Museum as well as my wife and me. Everyone at the
Museum, and especially Fro Rainey and Beth Ralph, have
been so kind that they have made us feel that we are part
of the organization, although, of course, we have no training
in archaeology or the modern techniques used.

For those who wish to visit Sybaris, there are other ways
than by the train trip which I have described. The quickest
way, of course, is by plane to Bari on the Adriatic coast, and
from there it is a motor trip of some 125 miles, the first 50
across the heel of Italy and the remainder along the shore of
the Gulf of Taranto. The Greek ruins at Metapontum may
also be seen on this route. Here the columns of a temple and
also the walls of other buildings are still standing and are well
worth a visit by anyone interested in the work of the Greeks
at the time of Sybaris. The direct motor road from Naples
runs for the first forty miles on a fine new autostrada which
will be completed all the way to Sybaris. Below Salerno a

detour can be made to Paestum, which should be seen if one is interested in what was built by the settlers from Sybaris; it will give an excellent idea of what must have been at Sybaris on a much larger scale. Beyond Paestum there are some ninety miles of twisting road through and along the ridges of the Apennines before one reaches the plain of Sybaris, a total trip of about 190 miles. However, by 1970 the magnificent autostrada will take the motorist within a very few miles of Sybaris.

One may also reach Sybaris by rail. The railroad runs along the coast from Taranto on the eastern end of the gulf to Reggio at the Strait of Messina. It is a two-car diesel electric, and I would advise not getting off at a station to stretch your legs. I did this, and when I saw the engineer return, I waited at the car step for the usual horn or call to get aboard. However, with one motion the engineer mounted the steps, started the train, and closed the doors. I was left hanging onto the handles while the train must have accelerated to one hundred miles an hour in five seconds. At least it felt that way. Luckily, Susy saw me, so I am still here. However, it gave me a point in common with Ernest Hemingway, who was caught elsewhere in the same manner and even carried through a tunnel.

There are other hotels in the neighborhood in addition to the one I have described. We stayed in one which was operated on an economical basis. The electric light was sufficient to see your way around the room, but under the best of circumstances reading for more than ten minutes was impossible. After a long day in the field this made an even longer evening in one's room. At this hotel, Susy, being a tea drinker, ordered tea the first day we arrived. We should have put our initials on the tea bag, for we were quite sure it was the same tea bag served at breakfast on our last morning. For any visitor to Sybaris I strongly recommend the Jolly Hotel (one of a large chain of hotels in Italy and Sicily) at Castrovillari, fifty minutes by motor from Sybaris: excellent clean rooms with bath, thoroughly modern, and reasonably good food.

As I have written, it would be hard to exaggerate the beauty of the site of Sybaris. At this point the shore line of the Mediterranean (Ionian Sea) runs almost north and south. The land for a distance of twelve to eighteen miles inland is flat with a few spurs of foothills, and the valley extends to a width of about twenty-four miles along the shore. Around this bountiful plain is a semicircle of magnificent mountains coming down to the sea at the northern and southern limits, the highest peak being over seven thousand feet. Snow lies on the mountains until late in spring, and the melting snow provides ample water through several rivers running to the sea. In the present day this water is skillfully used for irrigation; one sees field after field with canals running along each side, and the trees on the banks add great beauty to the landscape. In many places the rivers are lined with magnificent oleander bushes, blooming profusely. Some idea of the fertility of the soil may be gained from the fact that, as I have said, the farmers are cutting six to seven crops of alfalfa each year without any fertilization of the ground. The orange groves are a joy to behold. The soil is alluvial, having been washed down from the hills over countless ages, and it is to be presumed that this deposit has increased more rapidly since the cutting down of the great forests by the Sybarites and their successors. The work in the fields is still done in part with oxen having a striking similarity to those shown on the coins of Sybaris, and of a light color similar to that described by the ancient authors, who attributed the color to the magic properties of the waters of the Crati.

On July 22, 1961, Dr. Rainey, Signor Lerici, and two

members of his staff went to Sybaris. As previously noted, a group of Italian archaeologists had already excavated a small area in what is now known as the Parco del Cavallo, but the ruins here proved to be a Roman building in semicircular form with the remains of a few columns still standing. Near this building was a free-flowing spring of fresh water and, as work proceeded, a large shade tree near the spring afforded a lovely location for the daily lunch while working in the field. All the work done has been on the farms of the plain, and the fields of wheat and the pastures for the cattle provide no protection from the oppressive heat of the noonday sun. The farmers have been most cooperative and do not seem to object to the usurpation of their land, even to the extent of permitting the fields to be dug, although sometimes they do look as though they felt we were harmless madmen looking for the needle in the haystack.

At this time Fro felt that the long wall might be part of the city of Sybaris, and it was decided to pursue the excavation of this wall to its foundation as the first work to be done on a large scale. That July day was a long and tiring one, but the future plans were decided that night. Signor Lerici would obtain the permission of the Government to go ahead with the work, which would begin the first of September. Rainey left Sybaris the next day and was off to Cairo and then to Gordion and the coast of Turkey. From there he went to Tarquinia to see the work being done by Signor Lerici on the Etruscan tombs, and it was not until about the first of October that he came to Sybaris and concentrated on the long wall. The new proton magnetometer immediately showed its value, and in a few days the wall had been traced for over seven hundred feet. Digging was started at once, and the magnetometer proved to be accurate, as the wall appeared directly under the line shown by the instruments.

A letter from Rainey on the fourth of October conveys a clear and vivid picture of the start of a venture which was going to occupy a considerable part of his life for many years. He wrote (remember that this was an absolutely new, untried, and revolutionary method of archaeology in which he and Beth Ralph were the pioneers), "the Proton Magnetometer is a whiz at picking up the wall, and we have already traced it for two hundred and fifty meters. [A meter is 39.37 inches.] Test excavations began today and we have the actual wall at three points extending over 250 meters and are sure that our recorded anomalies are the wall. We have yet to learn the depth, height or width, and the significance, but this is now only a matter of digging. This afternoon we lost it near the Bruscate Road and are casting about to pick it up again and to determine by our magnetic soundings where and how it terminates. We will also follow it in the other direction.

"Miss Varrone, Lerici's archaeologist, and I are the guests here of the Muellers, a German-Italian family who run a large and highly scientific farm in the plain, but live in an ancient house in the hill town of Cassano. It is a kind of feudal setup and I have the feeling I am living in medieval times—even to the hospitality. They expected me to stay at least two months and quickly supply anything we wish—workmen, pumps, tools, etc.! Certainly this is not of the modern world."

A very important member of the expedition has been Enrico Mueller. Signor Mueller, of German extraction, is a tall, well-built, and energetic man, with a gentle voice and manner and an ability to win the good will of everyone with whom he comes into contact. He is a man of proven ability and has been of untold assistance to the expedition. Signor Mueller was constantly available for advice on problems of excavation in the difficult water conditions which developed and, if a tractor or additional labor was wanted for some par-

ticular job, he seemed to be able to produce promptly whatever was needed. He and Signora Mueller, a charming Italian
lady in her thirties, live in the hill town of Cassano Ionio, and
it was they who had originally suggested to Signor Lerici that
he try his instruments at Sybaris.

The road to their house winds up through the narrow
streets of the centuries-old town until you suddenly come
upon the façade, which for a moment appears to block the
street at the top of the hill. Inside, the house is spacious, with
high ceilings and seemingly endless rooms and corridors which
are filled with life by their six children and the servants. Life
in the house is so pleasantly informal that the guest is quickly
made to feel at home, not only by the host and hostess, but
also by the warm welcome of the children. Dining with the
entire family is an unforgettable experience, with the adult
Muellers seated opposite one another in the center of a long
table, working down in age to the younger children at either
end. The household provides the sensation of moving back
several centuries to a baronial type of life which has been
unknown in the United States, with the possible exception
of the great plantations of the South prior to the Civil War.
Signor Mueller operates a highly successful farm of about
1,600 acres in the plain some miles from his home, and has
installed all the latest and most modern equipment, at the
same time retaining some of the atmosphere of earlier days
by the use of oxen alongside the tractors.

The many workmen live in modern houses placed in
groups at various parts of the farm, and these little villages are
spotlessly clean and freshly painted. To any farmer, and even
to the layman, the fields are a joy to see; each one is enclosed
by its irrigation ditches along which are the magnificent rows
of trees with their roots in the water, thus not only adding
to the beauty of the countryside, but also providing the

needed windbreaks for the crops. Wheat, corn, rice, alfalfa, sugar beets, and oranges are the principal crops, and Signor Mueller operates a large rice mill where the rice is brought from the field, dried and cleaned, and then boxed to go to the grocery stores in Italy. The Holstein cows are beautiful animals, and there are some 350 in the herd. Everything seems to grow to enormous size, and I have never seen such magnificent pigs. Traveling amid the medieval or patriarchal society of this farm with its owner, I had the feeling that every workman and his family are known intimately, and there is a sense that the workmen have as much pride in the farm as does the owner. Signor Mueller has great confidence in the future of this area and of the value to it of the discovery of Sybaris. He and Mr. James Delmege, who has accompanied the Museum on more than one occasion as official photographer, have joined forces to construct a hotel and cottages near the shore, which they have named "Bagamoyo." There is already a delightful restaurant there on the beach, and some bath cabins. Nothing is more pleasant than a swim in the Mediterranean after a long, hot day at the dig, and then a good dinner with a bottle of local wine.

Both Signor Mueller and his wife have been interested in the problem of Sybaris for many years and have an intimate knowledge of the plain, the local landowners, the soil and water conditions. Had it not been for him, his standing in the community, and his diplomacy we would have had great difficulty in obtaining permission to trespass on the farmers' land. In obtaining water for his extensive farming operations, he has done frequent drilling and was therefore helpful in our drilling operations. Signora Mueller has already made a fine collection of fragments of early Greek pottery, all of which she had found in the neighborhood.

In the hope that we might find a few treasures such as

were in Signora Mueller's collection, Susy, Fro, and I went out one gorgeous October morning to the hill of Torre del Mordillo. This hill extends out into the plain like the prow of a ship and is probably about three hundred feet high, with the Esaro River circling the base. The sun was shining brightly and in the valley the mists from the night were slowly rising, but toward the sea one could look for miles over the cultivated fields and pastures for cattle. At the point of the hill stands a Moorish watchtower, still in perfect condition but roofless.

We approached the top up a gentle slope from the rear and luckily found that the plateau had recently been plowed. The surface of the ground was literally covered with broken pieces of ancient pottery, mostly in very small fragments and almost all of it of Hellenic and Hellenistic times. The best piece we found was half of a small vase, but I am sure had we made a thorough search, more would have been found, as there were many painted fragments lying exposed to the sunlight. We had been preceded by others, for there was evidence in many places of large holes which had been dug to extract pieces of value and interest. We did not have the luck of finding a lovely Tanagra-like head of a Greek goddess, many of which lie near the surface of this soil.

One of the most exciting moments of my life was a find I made on another day. At the excavation of the long wall we had been working with the power shovel, and each bucket of mud, with water dripping from its edges, was carefully deposited in a small row of mounds. As the bucket was emptied, three of us would get down on hands and knees and carefully sift the mud through our fingers to see if there were any artifacts and if the shovel was bringing up any pottery of interest. I was not having much luck when I suddenly felt a piece of what I took to be a rock about the size of a melon.

I took it over to a pump which was emptying water into a drainage ditch and washed off the outside mud. As it began to get smaller a sculptured stone showed through, and with a stiff brush I carefully cleaned the clay out of all the carving. Soon I was holding in my hand a small stone work of art of about 600 B.C. It proved to be a representation of the god Bes. He is extremely ugly, with a short, squat body, enormous head and belly, and long arms and legs. His tongue is protruding, and it is easy to understand how he was counted on to frighten away the evil spirits. It is somewhat harder to realize why he was also supposed to bring joy, unless it was as a clown. The back and sides of the stone are beautifully and smoothly curved. Presumably, he was set in the rim of a small, round fountain or wellhead, having his place between two gargoyles spitting water. If anyone who reads this has the good fortune to have a similar experience, I can promise you that it is thrilling and never to be forgotten. To think that a Greek, twenty-five hundred years ago, made this with care and skill, and that it lay unseen and forgotten, buried by twelve feet of dirt, for more than two millennia until it was in my hand. You may be able to appreciate the thrill and sense of reward for all the time, as well as all the disappointments, which the expedition has involved.

Any ancient sherd, tile, pottery, or sculpture which is found is immediately turned over to a representative of the Italian Bureau of Antiquities. It is carefully placed in a cellophane bag and is tagged with the information of exactly where it was found and in what stratum of soil it was located. I think that secretly the archaeologist must hope that every time an object is located he will unearth a beautiful vase or some hitherto unknown masterpiece of statuary, even in fragmentary form. However, since I was a complete neophyte and amateur, this small piece of sculpture was enough for me, and

Stone Representation of the God Bes

I can remember vividly the excitement and pleasure of the moment.

# XII

# THE INSTRUMENTS

The alluvial soil of the plain makes it a perfect place to work with the new instruments. They will discover any material under this soil, but if the soil is rocky or of a rock base it is impossible to distinguish between what is a man-made construction lying underground and what is the natural rock. Similarly, if there is magnetic interference, the instruments can be of little value.

It must be stressed in the strongest possible terms that, regardless of what may be found at Sybaris, the work done with the instruments which have been developed by the University Museum and Varian Associates of Palo Alto, California, will revolutionize the science of archaeology in any place where the nature of the soil lends itself to their use.

At Sybaris we started with the huge plain and then, by consulting the ancient accounts, we were able to narrow down the presumptive area to one which is between two rivers. However, there was nothing to tell us how far it lay from the sea, except that it lay in a hollow; and we did not know how much or how frequently the rivers had changed their beds, nor did we know which were the two rivers. At best we might arrive at an area of twenty square miles, and how impossible this would have been to explore by the old methods of drilling and digging, as the city probably lay from ten to twenty feet below the surface of the present-day fields. With the instruments, however, the archaeologist can walk across the fields, covering several acres each day and noting carefully any anomalies which may appear. (An anomaly is any type of material—stone, metal, or fired clay—whose magnetic quality differs from the magnetic intensity of the soil which covers it.) From these anomalies may develop a pattern of a building or even of a whole city, and it is then that the researcher will begin his digging. The work at Sybaris has proved these instruments. Since the first ones used in 1961 there has been constant perfecting of their accuracy and of their depth of penetration. With the latest one being used at Sybaris in 1966, objects twenty feet below the surface are located, and the instruments show whether it is stone, pottery, or metal.

The instrument which was developed and used by the Lerici Foundation in its original work in Tuscany was a resistance apparatus for measuring the electrical conductivity of the soil. The use of this was limited and the depth of penetration of the soil was not great, but it accomplished its purpose of finding the Etruscan tombs, mentioned at the beginning of this book. It was also used in the discovery of the long wall at Sybaris, but did not disclose any great length to this wall. This instrument was of little value in penetrating a wet soil, and the water table at Sybaris occurs in places at only about four feet below the surface and, as one proceeds downward, artesian forces are at work, quickly flooding any hole which is dug. In 1961 Dr. Rainey went to Tuscany to join Signor Lerici, and he took with him the new instrument, previously mentioned, made by the Littlemore Company. This machine was known as a proton magnetometer, and later that summer it was taken to Sybaris, where it was able to trace the long wall for almost a mile. It was able to penetrate to a limited depth but gave us our first hope of being able to locate the city. However, as the archaic Greek ruins were probably from twelve to twenty feet beneath the surface, the depth of penetration was still not great enough for anything but Roman remains.

It was not until 1964 that Varian Associates developed a new magnetometer, using rubidium. This could penetrate the soil to a depth of fifteen feet, but it was difficult to operate, as it had not been designed for the type of field work being done in Italy. Later Varian, in conjunction with the Museum, built an entirely new instrument using the element cesium. This magnetometer will record material twenty feet and more beneath the surface and is far steadier, more practical, and faster to use. (See the Introduction.)

I will try, as a layman, to describe my understanding of how the magnetometer operates. In the first place it looks like nothing you have ever seen before. At either end of an aluminum tube, about one inch in diameter, is fastened a can about the size of a giant economy can of tomato juice. One man walks across the field, carrying this odd-looking contraption. An electric wire runs from this back to a second man who is following some fifty feet to the rear. On this second man's chest is hung a viewfinder containing disks which have numbers around them like the odometer on an automobile speedometer. On his back are the batteries, and a wire runs from him to another piece of equipment set in the ground.

The instrument in the hand of the first man is the sensor of the magnetometer. In one can is cesium, and when an

*Using the Magnetometer*

electric current from the batteries is passed through it, it heats and becomes a gas. Simple so far, but now the electrons begin jumping between energy levels of the atoms. Don't let this bother you; just imagine anything jumping inside that can. The speed at which the electrons jump will be governed by the intensity of the magnetic field in the ground. In other words, if the magnetometer is carried over ground that has a stone structure beneath it, even though this is twenty feet down, the speed of the electrons will be slowed down, as the stone has less magnetism, and conversely, if it is over a magnificent Greek vase, they will go faster. The later magnetometers were so sensitive that in one spot they showed a large piece of iron lying on a stone floor.

Each field is divided into rows with stakes at either end of the row, the rows being fifteen feet apart. In the center of the field a sensor is fixed in the ground and an anomaly is placed below it. A reading is then taken, and the movable sensor is adjusted to correspond with this reading. When the man walks across the field with the other sensor, any deviation from this reading will immediately be apparent. The leading man takes two steps straight down the field and stops. The man with the view box then calls out the number which shows in his box, and a third man, carrying a paper marked off in squares, notes the number called. If we say that x is the reading of the fixed sensor and the number called is $x - 4$, we know that there is a stone beneath the spot, and if it is $x + 4$ we know that there is either a piece of metal or fired clay which will be found by digging. A hypothetical diagram will show exactly how a particular field will look after it has been fully surveyed. Each square represents six feet to a side. The upper diagram shows the numbers as they are read from the magnetometer in the field. The lower diagram has had the areas keyed to show the variations from normal readings of the magnetometer. You will see that when lines are drawn between the minus numbers it will show what we hope are the outlines of the Temple of Poseidon, the smaller temple of Apollo, the round Temple of Diana, and similarly with the plus numbers you have the arrows of Hercules and a magnificent tomb filled with pottery! The only trouble is that when you dig you will probably find that it is none of these, but the foundations of some fourth-century Greek structures which naturally could not be Sybaris. Of course, this diagram is a great oversimplification.

It was also necessary to have two drills of at least three inches in diameter which could pierce the soil to a depth of more than twenty feet. These drills were used for exploratory

| | | | | | | | | | | | | | | | |
|---|---|---|---|---|---|---|---|---|---|---|---|---|---|---|---|
| 0 | 0 | 0 | 0 | 0 | 0 | 0 | 0 | 0 | 0 | 0 | 0 | 0 | 0 | 0 | 0 |
| 0 | 0 | 0 | 0 | 0 | 0 | 0 | 0 | 0 | 0 | 0 | 0 | 0 | 0 | 0 | 0 |
| 0 | -2 | -2 | 0 | 0 | +1 | 0 | 0 | -2 | -2 | -2 | -2 | 0 | 0 | 0 | 0 |
| -2 | -6 | -6 | -4 | +2 | +8 | +2 | 0 | -2 | -2 | -4 | -8 | -4 | -1 | 0 | 0 |
| -6 | -4 | -4 | -6 | 0 | +1 | +1 | 0 | -4 | -2 | -8 | 0 | -2 | -8 | -6 | -2 |
| -3 | -6 | -6 | -2 | 0 | 0 | 0 | 0 | -4 | -8 | -2 | 0 | 0 | 0 | -2 | -8 |
| 0 | -1 | -1 | 0 | 0 | 0 | 0 | 0 | 0 | -2 | -6 | -8 | -2 | 0 | -8 | -8 |
| 0 | 0 | 0 | 0 | 0 | -2 | -2 | -2 | 0 | 0 | 0 | 0 | -6 | -8 | -4 | -4 |
| 0 | 0 | 0 | 0 | 0 | -2 | -2 | -2 | 0 | 0 | 0 | 0 | -4 | -2 | -4 | -4 |
| 0 | 0 | 0 | 0 | -2 | -6 | -6 | -6 | -2 | 0 | +1 | +1 | 0 | -2 | -6 | -2 |
| 0 | 0 | 0 | 0 | -2 | -6 | -2 | -6 | -2 | +1 | +6 | +6 | +1 | 0 | -2 | 0 |
| 0 | 0 | 0 | 0 | -2 | -6 | -2 | -6 | -2 | 0 | +1 | +1 | 0 | 0 | 0 | 0 |
| 0 | 0 | 0 | 0 | -2 | -6 | -6 | -6 | -2 | 0 | 0 | 0 | 0 | 0 | 0 | 0 |
| 0 | 0 | 0 | 0 | 0 | -2 | -2 | -2 | 0 | 0 | 0 | 0 | 0 | 0 | 0 | 0 |
| 0 | 0 | 0 | 0 | 0 | 0 | 0 | 0 | 0 | 0 | 0 | 0 | 0 | 0 | 0 | 0 |
| 0 | 0 | 0 | 0 | 0 | 0 | 0 | 0 | 0 | 0 | 0 | 0 | 0 | 0 | 0 | 0 |

| | | | | | | | | | | | | | | | |
|---|---|---|---|---|---|---|---|---|---|---|---|---|---|---|---|
| 0 | 0 | 0 | 0 | 0 | 0 | 0 | 0 | 0 | 0 | 0 | 0 | 0 | 0 | 0 | 0 |
| 0 | 0 | 0 | 0 | 0 | 0 | 0 | 0 | 0 | 0 | 0 | 0 | 0 | 0 | 0 | 0 |
| 0 | -2 | -2 | 0 | 0 | +1 | 0 | 0 | -2 | -2 | -2 | -2 | 0 | 0 | 0 | 0 |
| -2 | -6 | -6 | -4 | +2 | +8 | +2 | 0 | -2 | -2 | -4 | -8 | -4 | -1 | 0 | 0 |
| -6 | -4 | -4 | -6 | 0 | +1 | +1 | 0 | -4 | -2 | -8 | 0 | -2 | -8 | -6 | -2 |
| -3 | -6 | -6 | -2 | 0 | 0 | 0 | 0 | -4 | -8 | -2 | 0 | 0 | 0 | -2 | -8 |
| 0 | -1 | -1 | 0 | 0 | 0 | 0 | 0 | 0 | -2 | -6 | -8 | -2 | 0 | -8 | -8 |
| 0 | 0 | 0 | 0 | 0 | -2 | -2 | -2 | 0 | 0 | 0 | 0 | -6 | -8 | -4 | -4 |
| 0 | 0 | 0 | 0 | 0 | -2 | -2 | -2 | 0 | 0 | 0 | 0 | -4 | -2 | -4 | -4 |
| 0 | 0 | 0 | 0 | -2 | -6 | -6 | -6 | -2 | 0 | +1 | +1 | 0 | -2 | -6 | -2 |
| 0 | 0 | 0 | 0 | -2 | -6 | -2 | -6 | -2 | +1 | +6 | +6 | +1 | 0 | -2 | 0 |
| 0 | 0 | 0 | 0 | -2 | -6 | -2 | -6 | -2 | 0 | +1 | +1 | 0 | 0 | 0 | 0 |
| 0 | 0 | 0 | 0 | -2 | -6 | -6 | -6 | -2 | 0 | 0 | 0 | 0 | 0 | 0 | 0 |
| 0 | 0 | 0 | 0 | 0 | -2 | -2 | -2 | 0 | 0 | 0 | 0 | 0 | 0 | 0 | 0 |
| 0 | 0 | 0 | 0 | 0 | 0 | 0 | 0 | 0 | 0 | 0 | 0 | 0 | 0 | 0 | 0 |
| 0 | 0 | 0 | 0 | 0 | 0 | 0 | 0 | 0 | 0 | 0 | 0 | 0 | 0 | 0 | 0 |

Hypothetical Magnetometer Grid

work at any point where the magnetometer showed there were anomalies and also were used throughout the plain on a regular grid pattern to test the possibility of ruins. By 1968 more than 2,000 holes had been drilled over an area of many square miles. One of the drills was mounted on the back of a jeep, which gave it great mobility in moving from place to place. The other drill was suspended from a steel tripod. The auger of this machine was drilled into the soil by a portable gasoline engine fixed to one end of the drill. Drilling was done to a depth of twenty-five feet, and when that length was reached the drill was lifted by means of a chain hoist. When the drill shaft had been pulled from the ground, the earth was packed solidly around the flanges of the shaft. These deposits were then placed on a measured plank and usually contained pieces of pottery sufficiently large to identify the date. Comparing the measurements on the plank with the drill hole gives an excellent picture of the different levels of ancient occupation. By 1965 the region around the long wall was thoroughly drilled, and there were indications of a city, shown both by the drills and the magnetometer not far from the long wall. With the jeep-mounted drill of the Lerici Foundation a different technique, developed by Franco Brancaleoni of the Lerici crew, was used. Water from an accompanying tank was pumped into the drill hole as it was being cut, and this flushed out the potsherds. These were caught as they emerged from the hole, and a careful record was made of the depth at which they occurred. This method became so perfected that more than ten holes could be drilled in a day. By the summer of 1968, with better and more mobile drills, we were able to drill up to twenty-five holes a day.

The drill will prove several things. In the first place, it shows the various strata of soil through which we drill. The top will be the present topsoil. Then there may be some

*An Early Drill*

heavier soil below in which, in places, we will find Roman sherds. Next we will come to more good soil in which there may be late Greek pottery. Below this is a heavy layer of clay, and then we strike the good soil of the time of Sybaris. At this level we hoped to find archaic sherds and the walls of the buildings of the city.

In addition to all of this a very simple tool is used. This is nothing but a steel rod with a pointed end and a handle. It comes in sections of about three feet and can be extended to any depth for probing. It is called a *spillo* and is widely used by the grave robbers of Italy in their search for unopened tombs. With the Museum expedition it was possible to use it accurately wherever the magnetometer showed an anomaly. Two men grasp the handle of the *spillo* and put it into the ground. Water is constantly poured into the hole they are making, thus loosening the soil and sand and making deep penetration possible. In this way the exact depth and outline of any building may be pinpointed without the necessity of digging. The men using this probe become so skillful at it that I have seen them come to an abrupt halt and announce that from the feel of the *spillo* and the sound it is making they have hit a roof tile. This may be ten feet below the surface. With a few quick jabs they will pierce the tile and come to an empty space before going deeper to strike the stone of either a wall or a floor. This instrument, however, does not bring up any sherds in the way in which the drill does.

# XIII

# THURII

The history of Thurii is closely bound to Sybaris, for the people of Sybaris built it within a dozen years of the second downfall of their city. The discovery of Thurii will give us an insight into the former glories of the mother city and will be an important event in archaeology.

We know the city was moved in the year 443 B.C. by the former Sybarites to a site nearby and was renamed Thurii, probably on the supposition that the old name would bring continued ill fate and that there would no longer be the same hostility if it was not known as Sybaris. The founders of the new city were Lampon and Xenocritus, and this time they went about it in a way that would assure them help from the homeland. Ambassadors were sent to Greece by the Sybarites, to both the Lacedaemonians and the Athenians, asking them to help in the repatriation of the former inhabitants and in the founding of a new city. The Lacedaemonians officially refused their request and offered no help, although many from the Peloponnesus did migrate. However, the Athenians, who were then enjoying their golden age under Pericles, agreed to join in the enterprise.[118] It was still a land of fertility and wealth and held out great promise to any new settlers. The Athenians manned ten ships and sent them out under the command of the two new founders, and they also sent word to a number of cities on the Peloponnesus and offered a share in the new colony to anyone who wished to join in the voyage. Many people accepted the offer, in which the gods were again to play a part. They consulted the oracle and received a response from Apollo which is quoted to us as saying, "Water to drink in due measure, but bread to eat without measure."[119] We know that the land would provide limitless amounts of grain, so that when they arrived at Sybaris they set about finding the best source of water in accordance with the order of the god. Not very far from the former city they found a spring called Thuria which flowed from a bronze pipe which the natives called Medimnos (the Greek word for a measure of grain.) The fact that the bronze pipe was already there may indicate that this spring had also been in use by the former city. Thinking that this was the place which was indicated by the god, they built a wall around it and founded a city there, naming it Thurium after the spring. Today it is presumed that this may be the present Fonte del Fico,[120] from which the aqueduct runs; however, no ancient city which might be Thurii has yet been identified near the spring. They had brought with them the foremost city planner of the day, one Hippodamus, the architect of Piraeus and Rhodes. He laid out the city in squares, much as William Penn was to do some two thousand years later in Philadelphia.[121]

Lengthwise there were four great streets named Heracleia, Aphrodisia, Olympias, and Dionysias, and breadthwise and bisecting these streets there were the avenues of Heroa,

Thuria, and Thurina. The squares which were formed by
these streets were filled with houses, and we are told that the
plan and construction appeared good to them.[122] No trace of
this city has been found as yet and it too lies buried, so
that in the search for Sybaris it is equally possible that the
remains of Thurii may be found. Sybaris will be far the more
important, not only on account of its size and riches, but also
because it may tell us much of that earlier life of the Greeks
in the seventh century about which we know so little today.

In this new and promising settlement it was not long
before the usual internecine strife began. What practically
amounted to a civil war in the city broke out. The former
Sybarites were assigning all the most important offices to
themselves, and the land which lay near the city was appor-
tioned out in allotments to their families and friends, while
the less desirable offices and the land which lay farther afield
were assigned to the newcomers. The crowning blow socially
was the insistence on the part of the wives of the former Sybarites that they should have precedence in the offering of
sacrifices to the gods over the other citizenesses.[123]

When this division took place between the two factions,
the citizens who had been added recently to the rolls were
far more numerous and powerful, so that they killed practically all the original Sybarites and then undertook the rule
and further colonization of the city by themselves.[124] Even
this action did not satisfy the Thurians, and they now disputed with one another as to who should be known as the
founder of the city, even though the settlers were sent out
by the recruitment which Athens had carried on and the expedition had been made under the two leaders named by
Pericles. The Athenians were laying claim to the colony, on
the grounds that the vast majority of the settlers had come
from Athens; but opposed to this claim were the people who

had come from the cities of the Peloponnesus, who maintained that the colonization should be ascribed to them.
There were many individuals among the leading men who
were attempting to have the honor of being named founder
of the city. In this situation they decided to appeal to the
gods and sent a delegation to Delphi to ask the oracle which
man should be considered the founder of the city. In the
usual manner of the Greek gods, they were told that the god
himself should be considered as the founder. This apparently
settled the argument, for they declared Apollo to have been
the founder, and thereby they were released from any further
dispute and "returned to the state of harmony which they
had previously enjoyed."[125] It is in the Temple of Apollo in
Thurii that Justinus tells us are to be found the arrows of
Hercules on which depended the destiny of Troy.[126] In those
days there would not appear to have been any veto power,
and once the gods had spoken, everyone accepted the decision
and abided by it.

We have accounts of the life at Thurii, the wars and
the laws. The Thurians allowed their hair to grow long, wore
white turbans, went barefooted, and wore natural wool garments as white as those of Pamphylia but of a finer quality;
and they gave off an odor as though they had been steeped
in olive oil.[127] They soon found the country to be so extensive
and so rich that they encouraged large numbers of settlers
to come from Greece, assigned parts of the city to them, and
also gave them ample land. Those who continued to live there
rapidly attained great wealth, although not to be compared
to that of the Sybarites, and, with the recent example of the
fate of Sybaris before them, they concluded a treaty of friendship with Croton. They were apparently wise and experienced
in the affairs of government, establishing a democracy at the
outset. They divided all the citizens into ten tribes and gave

them names based on the nationality of their place of origin. For those three tribes which came from the Peloponnesus they gave the names of Arcadian, Achaean, and Eleian. For those outside the Peloponnesus the names were Boeotian, Amphictyonian, Dorian, Ionian, Athenian, Euboean, and Islander. One would have supposed that maintaining these individual entities would have caused further rivalry and discord, but after the original difficulties we do not hear anything more of disputes among various groups of citizens.[128]

They immediately drew up a code of laws for the government of the city, and these were written by the most learned man in their midst, one Charondas. We are told that he studied the legislation of other peoples to obtain the best practices then known, but he also developed several new laws and incorporated them in his work. It may be of interest, as showing the thought of the time, to mention some of the principles which he worked out to be incorporated in the laws. One of his first was that a man who had married twice should have no part in the counsels of the fatherland, for he believed that a man who brought home a stepmother to guide his children had planned badly and would do no better for the city. If a man was unfortunate in his first marriage and then made the same mistake a second time, he could not be regarded as having good sense. Men whose truthfulness could not be relied upon were to wear a wreath of tamarisk in order that all their fellow citizens should know that they had won this prize for their double-dealing. The result of this was that some of those who were made to wear the wreath committed suicide and thus rid the city of unwanted residents. The ancient authors say that this resulted in a complete freedom from the evil of false accusation.[129]

They forbade in their laws the holding up to ridicule on the stage of any citizen except adulterers and busybodies, which seems a rather unusual combination. They also wrote what was then a unique law which made it a crime to indulge in intimacy or friendship with unprincipled persons, and provided an action at law against such evil associations. They reasoned that characters of good men are perverted by their association with evil-doers and are led into deceptive pleasures which result in the eventual corruption of the good.[130]

They also found that, in changing from the former aristocratic government of Sybaris to the democracy of Thurii, the property qualification for honors was too high, and therefore the constitution was amended to provide for a lowering of this qualification. This was a first step toward universal suffrage and the right to property ownership. However, it took many more years for this to develop, and there were occasions on which the people arose and seized some of the land of the large landowners.[131] Another law provided that the generals, who might become all-powerful, could be re-elected only after an interval of five years. Some of the younger men who despised the civil authorities and wished the power to lie in the army attempted without success to have this changed so that a general would be elected for life.[132] Again we see that twenty-five hundred years ago there were exactly the same plots and difficulties that we still have in the numerous examples of the military's trying to take the government into its own hands.

Thurii played an important part in Magna Graecia, and it is apparent that the Thurians had developed a navy and must have had a considerable port, neither of which is mentioned in any way in connection with Sybaris. Xenophon[133] says that Phanosthenes of Athens in 407 captured Thurian triremes and imprisoned all the crews except the commander Dorieus, a Rhodian who had become a citizen of Thurii. Diodorus tells us that the fleet from Athens in 415, on its way to attack Sicily, put in at the port of Thurii and received every kind of courtesy. Appian[134] contains an account of the people of Thurii loading their ships with grain and sending them to the aid of the Romans under convoy of their own triremes. Athenaeus[135] mentions the pilot Euphranor of Thurii, and Cicero, in a letter to Atticus,[136] says, "I shall sail by the lower sea, and if it be difficult to start from Puteoli, I shall seek Croton or Thurii, and like a loyal and patriotic citizen play the pirate." That he safely reached the city is shown by a letter of his of April 10, 58 B.C., to Atticus which was dated from Thurii.

During the Peloponnesian War, Thurii took the part of Athens, which had done so much to help found the city, and Thucydides[137] contains an account of the Greek leader Demosthenes' sailing along the coast of the Ionian Sea until he reached Thurii—which surely indicates that there must have been a major port. At Thurii he found that the faction opposed to the Athenians had recently been expelled, and he therefore stayed at Thurii and gathered his forces for an expedition against Syracuse in Sicily. The Thurians were persuaded to join the expedition, but apparently with some hesitancy.

Thucydides also tells of ten Thurian ships under the command of Hippocrates[138] and again in 411 of five Thurian ships under Leon.[139] He mentions the Thurian sailors as though Thurii were a recognized seafaring city.[140] From all these accounts I think it a reasonable assumption to conclude that there must have been a considerable and active port. It is Dr. Rainey's opinion that this port lies within the area of the port of Sybaris which he has found.

One of the most fascinating and complex characters who took refuge in Thurii was Alcibiades (450–404 B.C.). He combined in his personality a man of noble birth, a playboy leader of the jet set and café society in Athens, a great general worshiped by his troops, a Lord Nelson as Admiral of the Navy, a traitor far surpassing Benedict Arnold, and a statesman who makes the double-dealing of Ribbentrop seem to be child's play.

Alcibiades claimed descent from the hero Ajax of the Trojan War. His father was killed in battle while Alcibiades was still a child, and Pericles was named one of his two guardians. In early life he became attached to Socrates, whose life he later saved in battle, Socrates having saved him in a previous encounter. He was a handsome, athletic, and vigorous man, a fine orator, extremely rich—in fact, one of the richest citizens of Athens—but he was inordinately ambitious and had absolutely no moral sense. He lived a life of wantonness and luxury, giving elaborate banquets, dressing ostentatiously, and delighting in walking through Athens in long purple robes which trailed the ground. At a youthful age he was made a general and immediately began secret negotiations with the Spartans, the foes of Athens. When he was about thirty-four, he urged the Athenians to attack Syracuse and thus conquer Sicily and add its wealth to the growing Athenian empire. At the time there was in Athens an older, successful, and more experienced general named Nicias, who was opposed to the expedition. Alcibiades was the better speaker and persuaded the Athenians to undertake the voyage. Shortly before they were to embark, the Hermes, small stone likenesses of the god placed before the doorways of many of the houses in Athens, were destroyed during the night. Those who were opposed to, and jealous of, Alcibiades accused him and his friends of the deed and also accused him of giving parties where he and his drunken friends acted out the sacred mysteries and mocked the gods. These two crimes, if proved, were punishable by death, and Alcibiades

demanded an immediate trial, but his position was so powerful that it was thought best not to delay the expedition which
had been decided on. He was given joint command of the
fleet and army with Nicias. This was to be the largest enterprise undertaken by the Athenians and the one farthest from
home. They sailed in more than 140 galleys with 5,100 men
at arms, 1,300 archers, and 30 horses—a ridiculously small
number of horses in view of the size of the cavalry forces of
Syracuse.

They landed safely in Sicily and soon took the town of
Catania, north of Syracuse. Shortly thereafter the opposition
to Alcibiades at home won the day. His wealth was con-
fiscated, and a ship was sent to bring him home to stand
trial. The guards sent to bring him back were told not to
arrest him in fear that his soldiers might revolt and free him,
so he was allowed to sail home in his own ship. Before leaving Sicily, he informed the Syracusans of the Athenian plan
to capture the city of Messina. Thucydides[141] tells us, "When,
however, they [Alcibiades and his followers] reached the
territory of the Thurians, they followed no further, but
left their ship and disappeared, being afraid to sail home for
trial in face of the existing prejudice." Thucydides goes on
to say that being now an outlaw, Alcibiades not long afterward crossed over on a freight boat to the Peloponnesus. He
was now, by default, sentenced to death in Athens. There are
further accounts of this episode in Plutarch.[142]

Alcibiades went immediately to Sparta, his former enemy, and, divulging the Athenian plans, persuaded Sparta to
aid the Syracusans. While in Sparta he gave up his luxurious
living in order to ingratiate himself, and he conformed to
their austere habits, with one noteworthy exception: He se-
duced the Queen, and she bore him a child. His mentality
may be judged somewhat by the fact that he still hoped the

King would put him in command of the army against his fatherland, Athens. However, the King naturally felt otherwise and ordered him killed. Alcibiades received word of the sentence and immediately fled to Persia, where his double-dealing became triple-dealing. I will not go into detail about his long series of deceitful acts. He persuaded the Persians to give only token aid to Sparta. When the Persians were to attack the Athenian fleet, he warned Athens. When the government in Athens changed, he was brought home from Persia and placed in command of both the army and the navy. He attacked and defeated the Spartan fleet in the Hellespont. He returned in triumph to Athens, where he was received in the Assembly and was crowned with a golden crown and absolved of his conviction. He was finally killed by those he had wronged, who set his house afire and stabbed him as he was escaping. Handsome, brilliant, able, wealthy, a great general and admiral, and not an honest bone in his body.

We have seen that the port of Thurii was considered an important one as early as 426 B.C., but the city itself was a stronghold which was the scene of constant warfare, both with neighboring cities and with the local tribes of Lucanians and Bruttians. About 390 B.C. Thurii was attacked by the Lucanians,[143] who also attempted to seize the port of Laus. Under the agreement then in existence between the cities of Magna Graecia, the Thurians called on their neighbors for help and rapidly defeated their foes. In 356 B.C. we read[144] of the Bruttians' capturing Thurii, and again in 317 B.C. an expedition of former Crotoniates left Thurii to attack their native city, but were driven off. In 302 B.C.[145] a Greek fleet from Lacedaemonia captured Thurii for a brief period.

That Thurii was a wealthy and famous city is shown by the fact that the first statue erected in Rome by foreigners[146] was one of Gaius Aelius, who had aided the Thurians in 289

B.C. and 285 B.C. when they were attacked by the Lucanians, and they presented another statue in 283 B.C. of Fabricius, who had aided them that year.

In the year 282 B.C. their neighbors from Tarentum sacked the city and drove out the Roman garrison which the Thurians had quartered there.[147]

There is frequent mention of Thurii during the Second Punic War. Hannibal, after the death of his father, Hamilcar, was in command of the Carthaginian forces who were then occupying Spain. The Saguntines and other Greeks in Spain had called on the Romans for help. Using tactics such as Hitler was to use with the Sudeten Czechs two thousand years later, Hannibal persuaded the tribe of the Turdetani to complain to him that the Saguntines were overrunning their country. Hannibal accused the Romans of stirring up trouble in Carthaginian Spain and, crossing the Ebro, he proceeded to lay waste the land of the Saguntines. Feeling that he could not only obtain glory by conquering Rome, but also prevent the Romans from attacking Carthage, he gathered a force of Celtiberians, Africans, and other nationalities. Leaving his forces in Spain in command of his brother Hasdrubal, he crossed the Pyrenees into Gaul and then made his famous passage of the Alps. Accounts differ as to the size of his army, ranging from 20,000 to 100,000 foot soldiers, 6,000 to 20,000 cavalry, and 37 elephants. The crossing of the Alps took place in the year 218 B.C., and not only was he struggling through the ice and snow over a pathless mountain, but his troops were constantly attacked and ambushed by local tribes.

A passage from Appian[148] is vividly descriptive of this march. "When he came to the Alps and found no road through or over them (for they were exceedingly precipitous), he nevertheless marched boldly forward, but suffered great losses. The snow and ice being heaped high in front, he cut down and burned wood, quenched the ashes with water and vinegar, and thus rendering the rocks brittle he shattered them with iron hammers and opened a passage which is still in use over the mountains and is called Hannibal's pass." In spite of this obviously slow method, Livy tells us[149] that they came to Italy in the fifth month, having crossed the Alps in fifteen days. (Some sixty-five years ago, I crossed the Alps with horses and a carriage, spending the night in St. Lazarus's room at the famous Hospice of St. Bernard, with six of us sleeping in one room. Today a tunnel carries automobiles through the mountains in a matter of minutes.)

Constant battles with the Romans ensued over several years, and in the year 216 B.C. Hannibal totally defeated the Romans at the battle of Cannae southeast of Rome and near the Adriatic Sea.

Appian says that he slew 5,000 Romans and took many prisoners, bringing the losses of the Romans in two years to over 100,000 men.[150] Hannibal offered to ransom the prisoners, but the Senate at Rome refused to permit any such action. This action infuriated the Carthaginian, who, as a spectacle for his troops, forced the Romans to fight one another, father against son and brother against brother. The remainder of the prisoners he put to death and, forming a bridge of their bodies, he passed over a stream.

It was not until four years later, in 212 B.C., that Hannibal reached the vicinity of Thurii and engaged in a major battle with the Romans at the neighboring city of Tarentum to the east. Tarentum fell to Hannibal by the action of a traitor who opened the gates at night, and the Roman garrison of 5,000 was surrounded in the citadel.[151] The Thurians attempted to help their friends, the Romans, by sending supplies in a convoy of ships, but these were all captured by Hannibal. When the Thurians tried to obtain the release of the prisoners, their envoys were persuaded to join Hannibal.

The prisoners were released and the city of Thurii was opened to the Carthaginians after the Roman garrison had been allowed to escape by sea. Hannibal conquered the nearby city of Metapontum and also won over the Lucanians to his support.[152]

Hannibal's star was now on the wane, and he was able to hold this territory only for about two years. He lost Tarentum in the usual way. The gates were opened by one of his captains who was in love with the sister of a Roman soldier.[153]

Hannibal retired to Thurii and sent to Spain for aid from his brother Hasdrubal, who crossed the Alps with fifteen elephants but was killed and his forces dispersed at Sena.[154] Carthage now dispatched reinforcements to Magna Graecia in one hundred ships, but fate was against them, and the wind drove the fleet to the island of Sardinia where all but twenty of the ships were either sunk or captured. The legend is that the Romans had devised methods to cope with the small force of elephants. Since the Roman horses were terrified of the sight and the smell of the elephants, the Romans mounted masts on countless oxcarts. At the top of each mast was a rotating log, and on either end of this log were fastened sabers. With the log revolving at speed the oxen were driven into the midst of the elephants, inflicting severe wounds. They also attached flaming balls of tar to the end of the log. They employed cranes that hurled heavy grappling irons, and even drove oxcarts in flames against their foes.

By 204 B.C., we find that Hannibal had a strong garrison in Thurii;[155] he evidently expected to defend the city to the end, as he sent 3,000 of the leading citizens to safety in Croton. This last desperate stand never took place, for the Carthaginians were being defeated in Africa by Scipio and in 203 B.C. Hannibal was called home. He constructed his own ships, but before he left he determined to plunder the cities which had become his allies. The Italians in his army who would not join him on the voyage were given to his soldiers as slaves, and any that were not wanted he slew with darts. He also killed over 4,000 of his horses and pack animals. This was his farewell after sixteen years of devastating Italy.[156]

Livy[157] sums up Hannibal's character by saying, "And I am inclined to think he was more marvelous in adversity than in success. For here he was, carrying on war in the enemy's land for thirteen years, so far from home with varying fortune, having an army not made up of his own citizens, but a mixture of the offscourings of all nations, men who had in common no law, no custom, no language, differing from each other in bearing, in garb, in their arms, differing as to religious rites, sacred observances, one might almost say as to their gods. Yet he somehow bound them together by a single bond, so that no outbreak ensued among the men themselves nor any mutiny against their general. Yet in the enemy's country, both money to pay them and supplies were often wanting . . . deficiencies which in the previous Punic war had given rise to many unspeakable acts on the part of the commander and soldiers. . . . Furthermore nothing was being sent from home, since they were concerned about their hold upon Spain, as though everything was succeeding in Italy." Polybius[158] adds to this that his army "was composed of Africans, Spaniards, Ligurians, Gauls, Phoenicians, Italians and Greeks, who had neither law, custom, speech nor anything else in common. Yet such was the skill of the general that, notwithstanding these great diversities, he made them all attentive to one command and obedient to one will, although circumstances were not always propitious."

In 194 B.C. the Romans changed the name of Thurii to Copiae. This name was used only for a few years until they resumed the old name, spelling it in the Latin form of Thurium.

# XIV

# THE EXPEDITION

It is not possible to work in the plain after November on account of the rains, and each year work has been discontinued from November until April. This left the winter months for planning, arguments, hopes, and dreams. I have often wondered how Howard Carter could bear the suspense once he had peered into King Tut's tomb. To seal it up and leave it for months, until the propitious time for reopening came, must have been an almost unbearable suppression of curiosity.

During the winter of 1961 and spring of 1962 there were two main problems to be solved. One was the perfecting of the instruments being used, but the principal one was how to overcome the unusual difficulty of coping with the influx of water. The water table is so near the surface that as the digging proceeds, the flow of water becomes greater. It is not unusual to see huge geysers of water well up in the center of the pit, similar to the bursting of a large water main, and the water spurts up in a fountain two to three feet in diameter.

This is called *sorgente* by the Italians. It was obviously impossible to dig under such conditions, and it was also dangerous for the workers on account of constant cave-ins. The possible collapse of ancient walls and the destruction of some priceless ruin also had to be avoided at all costs. The advisability of building retaining walls was discussed, but this was obviously too costly over any large area.

Fro went to Rome to discuss the entire problem with the Italian authorities and obtained their agreement to a long-term concession to the University Museum and the Lerici Foundation for the search and excavation at Sybaris, and it was determined to start work on the first of April, 1962. It was understandably difficult for the Italian archaeologists to accept the new and untried methods which were proposed, for not only did the Museum team expect to find a site by the use of instruments but also they were going to use a power shovel which in many minds meant possible damage to great archaeological treasures. Neither of these methods had been used before, but the Ministry of Antiquities was sufficiently broad-minded to accept the advantages of new procedures at such an unusually difficult site as Sybaris, and the permit was granted. There were also rumors that others might attempt to forestall our efforts and obtain authorization to excavate for Sybaris. We were told by the Italians that the finding of Sybaris would be announced in the middle of March and the site given as being near the long wall. Fortunately, Fro was able to forestall any such premature publicity, and no rival expedition developed.

At this time Dr. Rainey was insistent that the next step was to excavate, although Signor Lerici felt that there should be further drilling. There was little chance of the proton magnetometer's recording any of the anomalies at the depth reported by Dr. Donald F. Brown from the results of his drill holes, and there was a very real question whether a sonic device would penetrate that far. Actually it was not until three years later that the cesium magnetometer was able to reach the Sybaris level, although the Museum meanwhile had used the rubidium magnetometer with greater success than was achieved by the proton device. It was clear to Fro that the archaic Greek remains must lie from fifteen to twenty feet beneath the soil, and it was only through the use of heavy machinery that he would be able to reach them. The first search was to be made on the site of Brown's drill holes to determine whether the city lay in that spot or whether the sherds which had been brought up by his drills may have been washed there and there were no buildings.

It was decided to obtain a power shovel with a bucket of a square meter or more capacity. Again Dr. Rainey was willing to depart from the normal and use new methods which were called for by new conditions, in spite of many protests from fellow archaeologists who felt sure that this unorthodox method would destroy priceless treasures which lay beneath the ground. In addition to this, one bulldozer and some electric pumps would be needed. The entire plain below six feet is practically a lake in a bed of clay and sand so that constant pumping is necessary. The first year it was thought that two gasoline-driven pumps would be sufficient, these pumps having outlet hoses about the same size as those used by our fire engines. Two were quickly found to be inadequate, and unless the pumps were kept running twenty-four hours a day, the water rapidly rose. This meant much lost time, perhaps as much as a whole day, in bringing the level down again. Later on, five or six pumps were used, and the gasoline engines were replaced by electric pumps driven by an auxiliary generator, and these proved far more satisfactory. Even so, the workmen were often knee-deep in water and the effort of digging in the mud was great, and the results accomplished were slow in coming. Had there been no water in the plain the search for the city would have been greatly simplified and could have proceeded with great speed and a minimum of difficulty. It is impossible to stress too strongly the problems which have been caused by the water and the resultant delays and frustrations. At times the pumps became clogged with the mud and sand in the water, and at no time could the hand-digging be done in dry soil.

However, by the summer of 1962 hope was running high and perhaps something more than hope, a certain overconfidence. It did seem that with the success of the magnetometer in picking up anomalies and particularly its success in following the long wall, it was only a matter of using the power shovel and the pumps until the walls and temples of Sybaris would emerge from their years of mystery. Success appeared just around the corner, and on March 15, 1962, a newspaper announcement appeared in the Italian papers saying that the University Museum and Lerici had been authorized by the Government to proceed at Sybaris on April 1. Very appropriately, April Fools' Day. A quotation from the article reads, "The discovery of the Greek town of Sybaris by the joint effort of these two institutions may now be considered as a matter of time, since the prospecting equipment used has already proved to be capable of locating all the buried remains lying under the thick alluvial deposit covering the whole area. It appears justifiable to forecast success for this international cooperation." Reading this today, you feel that there would have been every reason by July to have tourist buses crowding the roads of Calabria to see the excavated ruins and watch the uncovering of great works of art.

To start the dig with the proper official good will, Ambassador Del Salto, Director General for Cultural Affairs in the Italian Foreign Ministry, gave a large lunch for the American Ambassador and Dr. Rainey, with many of the important Government officials present. Dr. Rainey was a long-time friend of the American Ambassador G. Frederick Reinhardt, with whom he had served in Ambassador Robert Murphy's office at SHAEF immediately after the war. This luncheon was particularly helpful, as there was considerable apprehension in the south of Italy about our method of work at Sybaris. However, Fro's effervescent charm, which can rival that of Charles Boyer, together with his scholarly accomplishments and reputation, as usual carried the day for him. His title of Professor of Anthropology and Director of the Applied Science Center at the University is regarded with esteem by the Italian scholars. Some newspapers approved of the methods to be used, and others were just as violently opposed. It caused a schism in the local Calabrian "Society of Friends of Sybaris," which was divided into anti-American and pro-American factions. However, once the work got under way, there was little difficulty and, quite the contrary, we always met with extraordinary kindness, politeness, and cooperation from the landowners.

Once the crops have been harvested on this rich agricultural plain, we seem to be able to go into the fields at will. Heavy trucks and drills, automobiles and station wagons, and finally the huge power shovel on its caterpillar treads were all brought in without objection from the farmers. In some cases we were working in the same field with cattle and horses and would have to keep chasing them away from the instruments and the wires crossing the field from the batteries to the sensors. Finally, when the long wall was being excavated by the shovel, a pit some twenty feet deep and over one hundred feet wide was dug to a length of over two hundred feet, and huge mounds of soil were deposited along the sides. It looked almost like a quarry. I know from experience how unpleasant some American farmers can be if a horse-back rider even tries to ride down a farm lane, but in no case have I seen or heard of any unpleasantness from the Sybaris farmers. We are always greeted with a pleasant good morning and a wave of the hand. It is a great tribute to the wonderful relationship which Signor Mueller has established with all his neighbors, and the expedition might have had untold difficulties if it had not been for his presence and help.

For the work to be done that summer, the Museum had five of its own people: Fro; Beth; Dr. Ellen Kohler, an ex-pert on the dating of pottery and sherds that might be found; James Delmege, who photographed the dig as it progressed and also the pottery that was found; and John Dimick for surveying. They also invited Dr. Donald Brown, who had done the previous drilling, to join them and contribute the benefit of his knowledge of archaeology and drilling. Of course, there was also a crew of a dozen or so workmen, the operators of the power shovel and the drills, and men for hand-digging. The Lerici Foundation had Franco Brancaleoni to oversee the operation of the jeep drill; B. Pastore and D. Gabrielli, geophysical equipment and drilling; L. C. Vanoni, archaeology; and Miss Marjorlein DeVos, a young and charm-ing Dutch girl who was studying for her postgraduate degree and who kept excellent records of the production of the drills. She was an accomplished linguist and kept us constantly in a good humor at the picnic lunches by her banter with the local workmen.

A large area was outlined near the long wall where the instruments, the *spillo*, and the drills had shown that there were stone buildings in great number beneath the soil, and numerous sherds had been brought to the surface. The build-

Excavating at the Long Wall

ings lay from ten to nineteen feet below the surface, and the sherds were found to depths of even twenty-five feet. We began the operation by starting to excavate along the wall with the shovel, expecting to go down to twenty-five feet, and it was thought that two pumps would keep the water out of the hole. Optimism was rampant and expectations were high; in fact, Fro felt that within a few days the theory that this was Sybaris would be proved.

In order to begin under the best possible auspices, the local Archbishop was present to bless the site. As the ceremony was completed, Signor Mueller, with his dry humor, whispered to Fro, "This is great, a Catholic blessing a pagan site which an agnostic archaeologist is about to dig up." As the work got under way, it was beautifully warm and sunny summer weather, and the fields were buzzing with activity: Fro directing the work of the shovel; Beth Ralph working with the magnetometer, surveying the fields for further evidence of buildings, and with the tripod drill making samples of the soil to be excavated. The jeep drill was moving from one hole to another under the direction of Franco, and it appeared as though results and new discoveries might be rapid.

At the noon hour the entire group would meet beneath the shade tree, not far from the Roman villa and alongside one of the many deliciously cold and fresh springs. Bread, freshly baked that morning, was brought from the country store at Sybaris together with bottles of wine, huge cheeses, and fruit. Nothing could have been pleasanter than this relaxed, friendly meal.

Three days after the start Fro wrote home to the Museum that "we have located with the proton magnetometer a large mass of considerable depth which looks like a temple base, and we will outline that and determine its depth with the drills and then calibrate the sonic device on that mass of known depth; the top of the wall is too shallow and too narrow to give us a good echo."

After only a month of work it seemed as though phenomenal success was very near and that it might be only a question of days before Sybaris was found—in fact, some were saying that it had been found. The shovel had dug a huge hole, the instruments showed a large area of buildings, and in the hole was a great deal of pottery of the seventh century B.C. One sure method of determining the site of the city is that any structure earlier than 500 B.C. must be Sybaris because there was no other Greek city in this area prior to that date. More of the pottery which was being found lay below eighteen feet in depth, which we then thought was possibly the Sybaris level. However, there were heartbreaking difficulties with the water, which entered the pit in far greater quantity than had been anticipated, and it was immediately necessary to obtain additional pumps. Even with four going constantly, the level was still so high that men working in the soil were digging in water. The pumps were continually being clogged with mud and silt, and each time one stopped, the water would rise. I remember one particularly disappointing episode. A Greek wall was just beginning to show in the excavation, and by the end of the day it was sufficiently out of water that it was going to be possible to uncover it the following day. We arrived at the dig the following morning to find the hole full of water. The night man had gone to sleep and failed to notice that two of the pumps had stopped, so all the work had to be done again.

Without any Roman walls in the upper levels to hold back the fluid clays and sands, the walls of the pit simply flowed into the cut, and excavating with shovels by hand below six or eight feet was impossible; there was no ledge or shelf upon which to shovel the dirt and mud as one went lower. During 1962 the greatest depth to which the power shovel could go was about eighteen feet on account of the water seepage. At that point the shovel struck a level of coarse, water-laden sand lying below a dense clay stratum. The closest analogy I can think of is the plight of a child building castles in the sand. When he builds too close to the sea, he finds that the seepage of the water constantly destroys his well-built walls, and they slowly melt away. This is to all intents what faced the Museum party in going deep enough to uncover the walls of Sybaris. Below eighteen feet the huge geysers of water, or *sorgenti*, under artesian pressure, welled up and flooded the excavation.

It must further be remembered that we were now working below sea level, so that there was no way of digging a drainage canal to the sea. It was decided to dig a deep pit, or sump, on the south side of the long wall, and this was done to a depth of about twenty-two feet. An opening was made in the base of the long wall, and the water flowed by gravity from the large excavation into the sump. From here it was pumped out and into irrigation ditches on the surface. This scheme worked well for a while, but at the fifteen-foot level the shovel struck a transverse wall which completely blocked the flow of water and, of course, there could be no question of tearing out this ancient wall or undermining it. This again left the lowest level in difficulty from water.

By May, 1962, rumors were flying abroad thick and fast. One enthusiast telephoned to America that Sybaris had been found, and articles began to appear in the news. In fact, I received a telephone call confirming the discovery from a friend at the Museum. The Italians sent down radio and television crews and were insistent on a story. Fro, not wanting a premature announcement which might have to be de-

The Long Wall

nied later, went to Cosenza and announced in Italian (and he will forgive me if I say that at the best he does not speak it freely) that there was now a good possibility of finding Sybaris in this particular area. He also went to Rome, where he, Signor Lerici, and Superintendent of Antiquities Foti held a press conference in which they gave the whole story, emphasizing that they could not say that they had found Sybaris on the basis of the archaic pottery which had been unearthed, and that the finding of the actual buildings alone would prove the existence of the city. I had always speculated as to whether this pottery may have been washed down from the site of the city, which lay further inland. When you see the power of the spring floods, the *torrenti*, and the size of the boulders which are brought down by the force of the water, vases or even statues could easily be carried for many miles. In summer these *torrenti* expose completely dry beds as distinguished from the rivers which flow all year. In the past these freshets might cover many square miles of plain with the soil from the mountains, but today they are kept within well-defined channels, so that no flooding of the fields occurs. Signora Mueller remembers that in her childhood the present rich farm land was a large lake in the spring of the year.

On one of the early days the shovel uncovered a huge Greek wall of the massive blocks which they used, but before any examination could be made to determine whether it was seventh or fifth century B.C., a *sorgente* broke through and covered the entire pit. It was many days before the pit was clear again and the wall was seen to be fifth century and no use to us. There were so many favorable factors that everyone felt we might have found Sybaris, but no one was willing to say so and, of course, the final word would be Fro's.

Ernesto Spina, the operator of the power shovel, handled

*Stratigraphic Digging*

it as easily and delicately as an extension of his own hands. He had provided himself with a whistle and, whenever he saw an impressive piece of pottery, he blew the whistle and then emptied the contents of the shovel at the feet of one of the Museum personnel. This helped to provide many valuable sherds.

In spite of all the difficulties, once the sump had been dug to the south of the wall, it became possible to dig a stratigraphic cut by hand on one side of the wall. This provided Dr. Kohler and Orio Miggiano, of the Italian Department of Antiquities, an excellent opportunity to determine the specific layers of soils, clays, and sands and to make a detailed study of the sherds which were found at each level. The work was done by digging down, on the edge of the pit, about six feet and making a wide shelf on which the workman stood. This process was then continued until there was a series of great steps to the bottom. On each step a workman could stand, and the one at the bottom would continue the excavation, throwing the dirt up onto the step above him, where the next man repeated the process and so on until finally a shovelful reached the surface. By taking a spadeful at a time, the archaeologist at the top may examine the clay for any sherds which it may contain, and thus determine the date of that particular level.

The long wall proved to be very puzzling. It was about eighteen feet high, and the instruments had picked it up for a distance of almost a mile, but as to what purpose it served the answer is still to be found. The upper part of the wall is of Roman construction with the south side, facing the Crati River, having a smooth and well-finished surface, suggesting that it was exposed and meant to be seen. The north side is unfinished and must have had an earth fill behind it. The lower part is of fourth-century B.C. Greek, made of large blocks of stone. The wall is too narrow to have been a city wall used for defensive purposes. It was at first thought that the wall had been built to protect a city either from the river or from a *torrente*. However, as the excavation went deeper, it seemed probable that the wall might have been built right through a Greek city. Why had the Romans added such great height to the top of the earlier structure? Further and more complete excavations may tell the story, but no conclusion can be reached at this time.

The second puzzle of this first summer was the apparently uniform layer of seventh-century broken pottery lying in coarse sand and below the ruins of the fifth century B.C. which showed in the pit. Because of this layer some Italian archaeologists felt that the site of Sybaris had been found, but Fro found it difficult to believe that the city could have been built on these sands and that nothing remained of the seventh-century B.C. buildings. Again the supposition was that these archaic pieces of pottery had simply been washed there. During that summer, drill holes turned up archaic pottery to the west and upstream from the excavation and in the clays above the coarse sands and in a stratum which appeared to be an actual living level.

The time of the permit from the Italian Government was running out; operations had to be discontinued at the end of June and a new permit obtained for the following year. It seemed a shame to stop with such possibilities ahead, and the results had been both meager and confusing from the point of view of finding Sybaris. A section of the long wall had been uncovered, a few fifth-century B.C. walls were disclosed, and a mass of sherds from the seventh century to the fifth century B.C. were turned up. No major building or piece of sculpture had appeared, and we were as far away as ever from the discovery of the city. From a scientific point of view, however, the results had more than justified all the time and effort which had been expended. The proton magnetometer had proved that it would be invaluable in proper soil conditions in any similar work undertaken in the future. It was a pioneer effort which had succeeded magnificently. Dr. Rainey, Signor Lerici, and Miss Ralph must be given the credit for having adopted modern methods in the field and for having discarded the old ideas and means which had been used up to this time. If nothing further was to be found, the summer of 1962 was a landmark in pioneering the development of an exact science in the discovery of the secrets of the past.

The work ended when several big blocks of the wall

collapsed into the excavation and caught a workman's leg beneath one of them—a possibility that had been feared all summer. The man was adamant that he would not lose his hip boot, and it was necessary to get Spina with the power shovel to pull him out. About two minutes after the man was freed, the whole wall collapsed and the dammed up water behind it broke through, filling up the hole; at the same time two of the pumps failed.

When the workman escaped, he was so overjoyed that he danced around the pit, and in his enthusiasm he fell in again, striking a ledge with his chest. This knocked his wind out, causing great consternation and tears. He was rushed to the hospital where the doctor effected a cure by painting his chest with iodine. The effect was immediate, and he went home all smiles with a great tale to tell.

The dig had now reached a depth of over twenty feet, and this was the end. There was general agreement on the probability that Sybaris lay further inland and that the following summer should be devoted to extensive work over a larger area with the instruments and drills.

The winter of 1962 was spent in endeavoring to obtain the permission of the Government to continue the work. What had been done received world-wide publicity in the fields of science and archaeology and was even being quoted by the Atomic Energy Commission as an example of what science could contribute to the humanities. It was now increasingly obvious that much might be contributed by a geological survey to determine the course of the rivers in ancient times, the line of the seacoast, and any possible settling of the land. We were fortunate in having at the University of Pennsylvania a distinguished geologist in Dr. Howard A. Meyerhoff, the head of the Department of Geology. Dr. Meyerhoff was immediately interested in the problem

Part of the Long Wall:
Greek Blocks Below, Later Roman Above

presented to him and agreed that during his summer holiday he would go to Sybaris and not only study the plain from the ground, but also survey it from a helicopter. His report was not completed, however, until after the work was finished in the summer of 1963, but it has proved to be of great value.

During this winter a great deal of effort was put into obtaining and perfecting a new magnetometer which would be sufficiently sensitive that it could locate objects at a depth at which we now felt convinced Sybaris must lie.

# XV

# SYBARIS, 1963

Permission was finally granted by the Department of Antiquities, and the Museum group arrived at Sybaris on the first of April, 1963, along with the scientists from the Lerici Foundation, who brought with them a magnificent new drill mounted on a car and capable of making as many as twenty holes in a day. Drilling was started further inland to the west of the previous site on both sides of the Crati River and north of the Coscile River just above its juncture with the Crati. The proton magnetometer presumably worked well, but to our disappointment not one piece of broken pottery was found. The area around the Crati was chosen partly because Lenormant had expressed such confidence that it was the site of Sybaris. The Roman aqueduct runs through this area on a perfectly straight line from the Fonte del Fico to the Parco del Cavallo, where the Roman house with the mosaic floor was found, so that there must have at least been a large town in the area of the Parco del Cavallo. As previously noted, the Fonte del Fico is considered to be the old spring where the gods had directed the location of Thurii. This spring flows freely the year round and would have provided abundant water for a city. Nothing was found south of the Crati River where I had always believed that Sybaris lay. It is possible that the Roman aqueduct is built on or over an earlier Greek one, but no evidence of this has yet been discovered. One drawback in starting as early as April was that the fields were knee-high in wheat and the sugar beets were beginning to show above ground; the owners, not unnaturally, were loath to have surveyors, cars, and drills going through their property. In spite of their reluctance they continued to be amazingly good-natured and cooperative and seemed to be as much interested as we were in finding Sybaris.

In the middle of April, Dr. Rainey's letter home gave a good picture of the situation and the difficulties. "Running this operation is just about as complicated as running the whole Museum with all its expeditions. We are sixteen people divided into four teams with four cars, two drills, a tractor and trailer and the electronic instruments—and we are spread over an area of fifty square kilometers! Next week we add two helicopters and a Roumanian. It would not be so bad if I could speak Italian . . . but the more excited they get, the less I can think of to say and the whole coordination, which is up to me, must be done in Italian. There are times when I lose a crew and don't know where they are or what they are doing. I have one little Dutch girl who is good at translation, but, of course, I can rarely find her. Orville Bullitt is convinced, by one Lenormant, a French scholar, that Sybaris lies at a certain point where the Crati river has changed its course and we are giving that a good try because he has me half convinced also—but it looks bad—the Roumanian thinks he has seen the ancient roads into the plain from the air so he is contributing the helicopters and an aerial map—but I don't see how roads twenty-five feet deep can show up from the air. Enrico Mueller, who supplies workmen, tractors, maps and the authority to mess up people, fields, etc. thinks it is at Doria, Senator Zanotti-Bianco thinks it is at Parco del Cavallo, the Princess Pignatelli is sure it lies at Apollinara, and I haven't the foggiest idea. If we ever do find this god damned city it will be an anti-climax."

Shortly thereafter Dr. Rainey wrote, "We have eliminated a great deal of the plain—endless empty holes! The puzzling part is that all the pottery found so far is in a quite narrow strip north and south of Casa Bianca [see end paper map] where we worked last year—perhaps the port of Sybaris or Thurii but not big enough so far for the cities. After using the probe [*spillo*] on several of the anomalies in that strip, I will select the best possibility and make another cut to twenty feet where archaic sherds are found in cultivated soil—not sand—and see what it is all about. Of course, any day we can hit the real McCoy inland somewhere. Metaponto, for example, has a port and then the city is a little distance inland. We are doing fifteen or sixteen holes a day to forty-five feet so you see we cover a lot of ground. Certainly we went deep enough in the Lenormant area because everywhere we go down to sand and that underlies the whole plain to an unknown depth. (Our maximum is seventy-five feet and still sand.)

"In brief, we have now covered practically all the area between the old courses of the two rivers, plus the Lenormant area, and find only that narrow strip of occupation in the general area worked last year. Damn peculiar! Well, there is still nearly two months to go and anything can happen. It's a hell of a big plain."

After three fruitless weeks of search in these areas the crews returned to a point north of where the work had been discontinued the previous year, and the drills immediately began finding archaic pottery from eighteen to twenty feet below ground level. This was all of the Sybaris era, but there were no great buildings and the question was again, Had these sherds been washed down from the city lying further inland in the path of the spring floods? In spite of the fact that everyone was thoroughly discouraged by the lack of any evidence in the past few weeks, we were glad to get back to land which at least contained sherds. Although aerial photographs showed faint indications of possible buried ruins in three places, one of these had already been drilled without results and the other two were equally unrewarding.

In May an entirely new area was explored, and for a time there was great excitement and hopes that perhaps Sybaris lay well inland and on an easily defended site in the foothills. I have already mentioned Torre del Mordillo where Susy, Fro, and I found Greek pottery in the fields, and it was this site that now drew the attention of the expedition. The farmers had told Fro of this hill and said there were the remains of walls all around the summit. It had once been reported as an Iron-Age cemetery. On examining this hill, we found masses of pottery, roof tiles, and building stones and the base of a huge wall some ten feet thick. Moreover, this wall appeared to run right around the edge of the plateau and could have been a part of the fortifications. The circumference was small for Sybaris, only about three miles around, but it had all the indications of an early Greek city and the farmers called it Thurio. Digging was immediately started, and the imaginative ones felt this might be Sybaris and Thurii or at least Thurii. It seemed much too easy—and it was. But you could picture this as a superb site for the ancient city, with the port down by the sea near the long wall and in the area where so much pottery had been found, the supposition being that this had been washed down from the city, and that the area in the plain was a swampy marsh at the time of Thurii. However, we knew from the ancient authors that the plain had been very fertile at that time and that malaria did not appear until much later. Also, of course, if there was any truth in Strabo's account it would have been impossible to flood this city on a hill, and furthermore we have been told by the ancient authors that the city "lay in a hollow." Later work here on Torre del Mordillo found some pottery of the sixth century B.C. and also a coin with the head of the Sybaris bull, but no large buildings were found, and all the buildings were of shallow depth and lying near the surface. After several weeks' work we finally decided this could not have been Sybaris, but a later Greek city.

What history this hill has seen! From prehistoric times down through the Bruttians, the Lucanians, the Greeks, the Romans, the Carthaginians, Spartacus, the Moors, the Germans, and finally the Americans. Did Hannibal perhaps stand here? Of what ruse was Alcibiades thinking as he was planning to escape? Was the little rise opposite the site of a villa where Cicero spent the days with his friends? Armies have battled across these fields for three thousand years or more, and we are still seeking the history and riches which lie beneath the soil.

Unquestionably Spartacus stood on the exact spot where we had been on Torre del Mordillo, as it commands the valley and he could have seen the flashing of the sun on the shields of the Roman legions advancing to wipe out his army of escaped gladiators and slaves. One of the great romantic characters of history, Spartacus was born a free man in Thrace in ancient Greece and, upon reaching manhood, enlisted in a Roman legion. Upon the defeat of his legion he was captured and shortly thereafter sold to become a gladiator and sent to the school for gladiators in Capua in Italy. These schools were heavily guarded to prevent any attempt at freeing the inmates, but Spartacus aroused his fellow pupils and plotted the disarming of the guards. With approximately seventy of his fellow gladiators the guards were overpowered and the gladiators fled to the slopes of Mt. Vesuvius. Here they were joined by other slaves and a small number of freemen. The Romans immediately took steps to capture them but, upon attacking the gladiators, they were badly defeated. This first success by Spartacus led many new recruits to his force, and thousands of slaves fled from their masters and joined the growing army in the mountains. Altogether at this time, about 75 B.C., he collected almost 70,000 recruits. With them he turned north and attempted to reach the Alps in order to cross over into Gaul. However, the Romans opposed his passage, and a pitched battle ensued in which the Roman legions were defeated and Spartacus, in celebrating the victory, sacrificed some 300 prisoners. Again he was besieged by recruits so that shortly thereafter he began a march on Rome with an army of 120,000. Although he defeated the Romans in another battle, it evidently weakened his forces, for he abandoned his march to the north and turned south, crossing the Apennines until he reached Thurii, where he captured the city.

Installed in Thurii, he anticipated further attempts by the Romans to subdue this uprising of the slaves and to prevent their fellow slaves from joining them in this haven from the oppression of their masters. The whole way of life and economy of the Romans would be threatened if the slaves were able to desert the farms and households. Spartacus forbade trading in gold or silver in the city but encouraged the accumulation of brass and iron, which would be of use in the battle he expected. Looking at this peaceful plain today, one can picture how this throng of more than 200,000 stalwart men must have spread outside the walls of ancient Thurii where Spartacus had his headquarters. He ruled his army with an iron hand, training it daily, and again defeated a small force of Romans. By this time the fear in Rome had become so great that it became impossible to find a leader willing to stake his future by attacking Thurii. Finally Licinius Crassus volunteered to accept the Praetorship and marched south with six legions in 71 B.C. On arrival, Crassus promptly attacked and killed 7,000 of the army of Spartacus. Spartacus then left the city in an attempt to escape to the west and cross over into Sicily. However, his forces were surrounded by the Romans, who enclosed them with a wall, a ditch, and poling. Spartacus endeavored to burn the poling by throwing lighted faggots in front of it, but the Romans held firm and in a pitched battle slew 12,000 of their opponents. The Roman account of this battle has a slight similarity to our own reports from Vietnam, for we are told that their total losses on this day were three killed and a few wounded. In order to instill courage into his followers and to show them what might be expected in case of defeat, Spartacus crucified a Roman soldier in full view of both armies.

The army of Pompey was in Spain and on its way back to Rome. The Senate immediately ordered him to march to Thurii to reinforce the battling legions. There was great jealousy between the various Roman generals, and Crassus was loath to have Pompey obtain any credit for a victory, since Crassus had already administered a severe defeat to Spartacus. On hearing the news of Pompey's approach, Crassus immediately issued orders for an attack.

Spartacus now asked for peace negotiations, which were spurned by Crassus, and a long and fatal battle took place. Spartacus was wounded in the thigh by a spear. He could no longer use his leg, so he continued to fight on one knee, holding his shield in front of him. He was finally slain, and in the carnage which followed his body was not found among the dead. The Romans took six thousand prisoners whom they marched to Capua, a few miles north of Naples, and Pompey received credit for the triumph. These prisoners were crucified along the road all the way from Capua to Rome. Thus ended a gallant revolt by a brave man and closed a picturesque chapter in this exciting and blood-soaked plain of Sybaris.[159] In this vast treasure hunt, who will be the one to find the shield of Spartacus?

Meanwhile, Dr. Meyerhoff had made his thorough study of the site by land and by air and had written a painstaking report on the geologic factors affecting the search for Sybaris. His report said that no conclusive evidence of the old deltas of the Crati and Coscile was found. The modern delta probably has been built forward more than a mile since Greek occupancy. He stated that the long wall and the Roman villa at the Parco del Cavallo suggest subsidence, for the top of the Greek section of the wall is approximately at sea level, the base being nearly six feet below. For the villa a minimum of seven and one-half feet of subsidence is indicated since the structure was built and occupied. Examination of sixty miles of shore line eliminated the possibility of any regional subsidence within historical times; hence the sinking of the wall is a local phenomenon. He went on to say there is no reason to believe that upstream localities were affected for more than a mile or two. Burial of Sybaris was, then, a fluvial phenomenon. Only solid wall and rock structures might be left standing, and the remains would consist chiefly of foundations, tombs, and columns, together with pottery and any small or heavy objects likely to thwart or escape the power of flowing water.

The wall which was unearthed Dr. Meyerhoff believed

to be a retaining wall at the mouth of one of the rivers. If this supposition is correct, the Crati has built its delta forward a mile and a half, or slightly more, into the Gulf, and he concluded that the maximum depth to which structures and artifacts of Greek derivation might be expected is twenty feet plus.

He further thought that any remains of the Greek city should be encountered within twenty-five feet of the surface at the junction of the Coscile and Crati Rivers and might deepen to over thirty feet upstream to the confluence of the Esaro. Northward along the railroad the depth of burial should diminish, and eastward at the town of Sybaris it might not exceed twenty feet.

Dr. Meyerhoff went on to suggest that the records indicated that the drilling may have stopped short of the optimum depth at which finds might be expected, and recommended that holes about twenty-five feet deep should be drilled from south of the Sybaris railroad station and on either side of the tracks. He further believed that the physical characteristics of Torre del Mordillo made it improbable as a site for Sybaris.

He concluded that many square kilometers now lie south of the Crati River before it reaches its confining delta terrace, and all of this land lies north of the meander scars of the old river and could well have provided the site for Sybaris. Therefore, renewed attention should be given to the flood plain southeast and south of the Crati.

At the end of the summer of 1963 the conclusion reached was that the area around the long wall was the ancient port of Sybaris and Thurii, and might prove to be Sybaris itself. However, from the hundreds of drill holes in this area very few structures were located, although in the area around Lattughella, north of the long wall, there might be some of the foundations of Sybaris. Torre del Mordillo was discarded as too small to have been the site of Sybaris, but it might prove to be Thurii. One additional problem presented was that the Italian archaeologists believed that the Sybaris pottery found in the long wall area all showed signs of having been washed down by floods. Aerial maps faintly indicated old roads converging at the point where the rivers now meet, but drilling in this area and also south of the Crati brought minor results.

We ended the summer of 1963 by concluding that the many large stone structures picked up by the magnetometer, and struck with the *spillo*, in an area of about four square kilometers around the long wall were probably the remains of the port. It is almost certain that at the time the shore line was close to these ruins, although today the sea lies a mile and a half to the east. Although the excavations had produced only ruins of the fifth and fourth centuries B.C., the indications were that this was the oldest part of the site, since here pottery was found above the level of the sea and in levels of human habitation and was not buried under later Greek and Roman deposits. It was also determined by test digging further inland at the Fonte del Fico that the remains were all Roman and did not contain any earlier Greek work.

# XVI

# ARCHAIC BUILDINGS FOUND AT LAST, 1964

I n spite of having no definite proof of the location of Sybaris, we left for home in the fall of 1963 with high hopes that we were approaching the solution. The number of buildings which had been located, the prevalence of Sybaris pottery fragments, and the continued improvement in the magnetometer led us to the conclusion that, if we continued north of the site worked on during the summer, we were sure to strike important ruins. Admittedly we had little real evidence that we were nearing the city, but optimism must be dominant if this type of search is to succeed. We had the optimism, the skill, the technical knowledge, and the determination to go ahead. All we needed was a bit of luck.

During the winter there were again published stories that Sybaris had been found with virtual certainty, and the Italian Government talked of draining the site if the archaeologists would delineate the area under which they believed the city lay.

Difficulties again rose over obtaining permission to continue the work, and much concern was felt as to whether the authorities might forbid the Museum to do any further excavation. The difficulties were finally resolved, and we were able to make plans for the summer of 1964, which we all hoped would prove to be the year of discovery. It was proposed that the Museum would put at the disposal of Professor Foti all its equipment and instruments, furnish the personnel needed for the operation, and furthermore finance the excavations planned for May. This would satisfy the Italian authorities, as the work would be under their supervision. Fro and Beth, of course, would continue to be on the site. It was this kind of paper organization to which approval was finally given. Sometimes I think that more time and worry have gone into the continuing struggle to obtain the right to search than have gone into the actual search itself. It was not until April that Professor Foti, in charge of the archaeological work in the Calabria area, gave his approval to this plan, and it was decided to concentrate the work in the Lattughella area about one kilometer northwest of the long wall. Dr. Rainey believed there was no question that this area was at least the port of Sybaris-Thurii, and might well be the city itself.

Final approval came too late for the spring work, and it was not until the twenty-second of July that a telegram arrived telling us that permission was granted.

After the disclosure of the effectiveness of the camera used in the ill-fated U–2 airplane over Russia, it occurred to some of us that it might be possible to use a similar camera to advantage at Sybaris. We had already examined carefully the complete aerial photographic survey of the plain, but from what we read in the newspapers, the U–2 camera, as we called it, was able, by some still secret method, to disclose under-

ground structures. Inquiries were made of the Itek Corporation of Lexington, Massachusetts, the developer of this
camera, as to whether they could photograph an area of about
one hundred square kilometers. In our innocence it seemed
simple enough. We would furnish the plane and they the
camera. The fact that it was a "secret weapon" did not enter
into our original thinking, but we quickly found out that both
the United States Government and the Italian Government
had serious reservations. However, both authorities were most
sympathetic when the problem was explained to them and
gave us their wholehearted cooperation. Unfortunately, it was
not until two years later, in June, 1966, that everything was
arranged for the photography which we thought might give
us an important clue, although we did not place too much
hope in the result on account of the depth of the soil which
over the centuries has accumulated above Sybaris.

The summer of 1964 was spent in working with a new
magnetometer developed by Varian Associates, using rubidium. This gave better results and deeper penetration than the
old proton one, and some interesting archaic pottery was
found to the north of the long wall. We worked further inland with the two drills, but practically everything discovered
dated from Roman times. A letter from Rainey at this time
(October, 1964) gives a good picture of the work. "The new
rubidium magnetometer is really a whiz! One guy walks along
with a thing that looks like a vacuum cleaner and our fellow
from Varian operates a whole bus load of gadgets. When we
pass over a buried building the loudspeaker screams so you
can hear it for at least half a kilometer. That crew is busily
exploring the so-called port area toward the sea (northwest of
the long wall), and they have found a whole mess of ruins
which are certainly Roman. The drills are proving them to

beat the band. We are digging down to an archaic structure at the northern end, but as usual are having a hell of a time with the pumps."

Beth Ralph's instruments finally picked up significant buildings. She was fortunate in having with her Dottoressa Paola Zancani Montuoro. Signora Zancani's advice was that there was more than ample evidence of a complex of archaic structures, and that the work should stop on account of the danger of destroying something of value. It was then November and the rains would come shortly so that there would not be time to do a careful hand excavation. One of the problems was that there were so many structures that it was hard to find a place to make a deep sump hole for the pumps to use. The buildings lay about twelve feet below the surface. Burned clay and roof tiles were found which were unmistakably of the Sybaris era. These tiles are over a foot long and about eight inches wide, extremely heavy, and must have necessitated strong construction for the support of such a large roof. In addition large stones appeared, not cut in a rectangular fashion, but appropriately selected for a significant building. There were also potsherds, all archaic and none of any later date. It was a difficult decision to make to close down for the winter, with a building of Sybaris just below us and needing only a few weeks' more work to prove the discovery. However, the group packed up and looked forward to the spring when Sybaris would surely be found.

The reasons for stopping may best be given in the words of two of the experts who were working there. One of them reported, "First thing this morning I went to see the excavation supervised by a man with mud up to his ears. I feel that I should say that you have the most complete and convincing evidence: structures (several walls to be felt, not seen), sherds, roof tiles, definitely all sixth century B.C. The important fact seems to be there are no later remains above the archaic ones. In such conditions it would honestly be a crime to carry on work with the few hopes of picking up more evidence (what more?) and with the inevitable consequence of damaging what can still be preserved in the depth . . . I advised them to stop that terrible engine!"

The other expert said, "When the archaeologist came and saw—or rather knew—how many walls there were, we [decided] immediately we could not possibly consider making a 'poggo' for the 'cipolle' of those damn pumps. We were too near a structure—perhaps a complex of structures—which the rubidium magnetometer could pick up. If we had wrecked anything it would have been awful archaeologically, and politically, of course, even worse. The sherds associated with the structure are wonderful, all archaic, one or two pieces of Corinthian. The roof tiles are archaic too. All in all, a date in the first half of the six century B.C. (which is just the time of Sybaris). If this is not Sybaris then the people who lived in this complex of archaic structures certainly knew where Sybaris was."

Fortunately, at this point we had agreement with the Italians that there would be no publicity about what seemed to be certain success in the long search for the great city of Sybaris. Fro had wisely taken the position that he would agree to no announcement until actual seventh-century B.C. buildings had been uncovered and the outline of the city delimited.

I suppose that, fundamentally, anyone engaging in this type of work must be an optimist. When I think back over the years of plans, hopes, hard work, discomforts, great and exuberant expectations of success being just under the next spadeful of earth and then heartbreaking disappointment when the discovery is a fourth-century stone instead of a sixth-century, I wonder why one kept on. We are really children on a treasure hunt on a grand scale, the only difference being that the children are now grown up and carry on their search with spades, magnetometers, drills, and power shovels.

In November of 1964, Fro issued a press release in the United States on the work which had been done at Sybaris during the summer and was very careful to mention that it was all done under the supervision of the Italian Government. He also gave credit to the Lerici Foundation, which in reality was taking a continually smaller part and interest in the work, only occasionally sending one or two men to see what was being accomplished. Unfortunately, when this release was sent to Europe by the press association, no mention was made of the Italian Government authorities or Lerici. This, naturally, created great difficulty for the Museum, as the Italian newspapers carried, in the words of an Italian official, "the sensational news of a discovery of Sybaris by an American Archaeological Mission." Fro had, of course, not claimed the discovery of Sybaris, but the power of the press for harm is infinite. Once the "news" is out, the denial, if the press will print it, is in two lines on the last page. The Museum was immediately told by the Italians that the story was contrary to scientific fact, and prejudicial to the Italian antiquity services and to their national dignity, and, of course, the Italians were entirely correct in making this statement. They kindly went on to say that they realized Dr. Rainey was not in any way responsible, but that as a result of the situation, it was very unlikely that the Museum would obtain a favorable decision regarding further concessions for work at Sybaris, and that it would be expedient for the Museum to choose another locality for its research in Italy. I immediately secured copies of Fro's original statement and a copy of what was sent to Europe by the press association. In securing the

one from the press bureau, I naturally disclosed why I wanted
it. I soon learned that I should not have made this disclosure,
for a few days later I was amazed to have Fro phone me that
he had an inquiry from Rome from a press agency asking him
for a statement on the difficulties the Museum was having
with the Italian Government. When I spoke to the agency
representative about this and asked them please not to make
things any worse than they already had by their failure to
quote Dr. Rainey's credit to the Italians, I was told that news
was news, good or bad, and must be printed. Fortunately, so
far as I know, nothing more appeared in the Italian papers.
After a great deal of diplomacy, we obtained permission to
return to Sybaris in the summer of 1965.

At this time the Museum had under way a monograph
on the work at Sybaris, and Fro very kindly asked me to provide all the obtainable quotations from the ancient authors
who mentioned either Sybaris or Thurii. Eventually I found
close to eighty authors in this category, most of whose works
are obtainable in English translation. For those in the original
Greek, I was helped by Christopher Black and Elissa Wan-
tuch, graduate students in Greek at the University, who provided the translations. From these quotations, at Fro's request, I also wrote a memorandum on where I thought
Sybaris might be located, using the ancient authors' account
to reach my opinion. My conclusions in the article were that
the long wall, excavated in 1962, might be part of the port
of Sybaris, and that the broken pottery found there had been
mostly washed down from the city, which lay further inland.
I further stated, "That this site was a port, and not the city
itself, may be accounted for by Procopius, who writes in his
*Bellum Gothicum,*[160] 'Not far from these passes, on the coast,
is Rusciane, the naval harbor of Thurii.' That the city lay
inland is indicated by the fact that the wine was sent in pipes

to the seashore and part of it sent over to the city by boat. A possible further indication that the city was not on the sea is contained in Livy. Hanno, in 212 B.C., attacked Thurii, which was built near Sybaris, after the latter's destruction. Marcus Atinius was in command at Thurii, but escaped. Livy's words[161] are 'Atinius and his men were brought down to the sea and ships.' The city lay in a hollow[162] and was therefore not as far inland as the foothills. However, as grapes were cultivated in the hills, it is possible that the city lay within easy reach of the vineyards for the daily work. Since the city lay between the rivers, and the Sybarites prided themselves on growing to old age at the bridges of their two rivers, we should look for a location where the rivers were reasonably close together. The city walls were possibly five to six miles in circumference. If the rivers were within, or close to, the walls of the city, then a place where the rivers were about two miles apart would be a logical spot. Dr. Meyerhoff has examined the ground carefully and has also surveyed it by helicopter. He believes it to be likely that at that time (600 B.C.) the rivers could have been about three miles apart at a point five miles inland from the present shore, and he believes it is possible that the Coscile could have used its present bed, and that the Crati could have been a mile or more south of its present bed.

"Following up these theories, taken largely from the works of the ancient authors and not based on scientific evidence, it would seem desirable to search for Sybaris on the south bank of the Crati river, at a point five to six miles inland, and also examine the area between the rivers at this point."

The area described here is between four to five miles inland from the work that was in progress at the long wall, which lay north of the river, but no significant anomalies had been found in this area further inland. Some weight must also be given to Athenaeus's statement[163] that the sea stretched beside it.

The discovery of Sybaris in 1968 showed how wrong I was and how dangerous it is to deduce facts from the vague ancient accounts.

# XVII

# "WE HAVE FOUND
# SYBARIS," 1965

Owing to the great difficulty of getting the water out of any pit which was dug, a consulting engineer was now employed, a man of world-wide experience in such problems who had acted as consultant on the construction of many large dams. Robert L. Raikes made a complete study of the site and submitted a report in February, 1965. It was his thought that the clear distinction between the sea sands and the sand which had been washed down by the Crati River could be seen at the mouth of the river, and that the bands of clay and sand indicated the prior existence of a lagoon into which the waters of the Crati were discharged. If such a lagoon did exist, then a sudden inrush of sea water seemed explicable only in terms of a cataclysmic (but not necessarily very large) sinking of the coastal strip. The downward movement may have taken place in a number of separate occurrences, but it must be supposed that the first occurrence would have largely destroyed the settlement if it was still in existence or have removed much of its ruins if it had already been abandoned. It seemed reasonable, according to Raikes, that the settlement, whether it was Sybaris or a port, would be found only on the buried mound of sand. The reason for this was that the existence of masonry structures would have protected the dune material on which the settlement was built from total removal by the marine transgression. It appeared to him that the earliest levels of Sybaris might be largely obliterated by sea action, and he emphasized that this explanation made the discovery of any large part of the ruins unlikely since, although these ruins would have served to delay the erosion of dune material on which they were built, they would have suffered considerably themselves in the process. He went on to say that the Roman aqueduct which points directly to that part where the buried mounds are still above sea level suggests a small inland settlement in Roman times to which water had to be piped because of lagoon conditions.

Raikes stated categorically that the method in use of excavating and pumping could not possibly succeed. The water in the underlying sand is under a subartesian pressure, which is why excavations up until this time have all been flooded from the bottom by running sand. He recommended that the most effective way of dewatering an area selected for excavation would be by means of a well-point system inserted after excavation of the top six feet of soil. This system would, according to Raikes, effectively lower the water table to a depth of over twenty feet and permit reasonably effective hand-digging after the power shovel had removed the top surface.

Beth Ralph returned to Sybaris in May of 1965 with the expectation of using a new magnetometer which had been developed during the year by Varian Associates and which would employ the element cesium in place of rubidium. Un-

fortunately, certain difficulties had been encountered in perfecting it, and it was not finally available until later in the
summer. The Museum was anxious to do more work with the
magnetometer at the site where archaic sherds had been
found the previous fall, and if sufficient evidence appeared, to
excavate a test pit. Estimates were obtained for using the
"well-point" method recommended by Raikes, but until there
was more evidence, the cost seemed excessive for the results
which might be obtained. We all felt very optimistic about
the results which would be forthcoming in the summer: we
had definite evidence of archaic sherds; the aerial photographs
were to be made in April; a new and more powerful magnetometer would be available; a possible way of conquering
our nemesis, the abundance of water, had supposedly been
found in the well-point system; and our difficulties in getting
permission from the Government were finally overcome. By
March, I was writing Fro in Rome that I would expect him
to bring me home one of the arrows of Hercules, said to be
at Sybaris. The hopes were that there would be sufficient evidence to warrant a small test pit's being dug in June at the
location where work had ended in the fall, and that Professor
Foti would be on hand to give his supervision to the work and
to be assured that no archaic structures were damaged.

Few people realize the activity of those who are engaged
in this type of work. They move from one site to another as
the seasons require. In the spring, Beth, having been at Helice
in Greece, was in Turkey at Gordion, seeking tombs and walls,
leaving in a month for Paestum where she would work at
the Sele looking for buildings, then returning to Sybaris with
further plans to go to South Carolina to look for a revolutionary
fort. Raikes was in Rome on his way to Beirut, Jordan, Sudi,
and Gordion; while Fro was on his way to Sybaris, stopping
off at digs at Ischia and Bolsena. The following year he came

The Constant Battle Against Water

to Sybaris from three weeks in the Libyan Desert, where the temperature ran to 115 degrees. No armchair professors these.

Work began the first of June, 1965, at the site where we had stopped digging in the fall. A letter from Fro gives a clear picture. The weather was beautiful, clear and sunny, with the plain a mass of color from the spring rains and the days not yet having reached the scorching heat of midsummer. Fro said, "We started with six workmen and began pumping with four electric pumps (we had our own portable generator). By Saturday afternoon we had the water down to about a foot and a half deep all over the huge hole, with one big gasoline pump standing by in case of failure of one of the electric pumps. Two men stay on all night to keep them going and to clear them when they get plugged up with silt. This morning Engineer Garrone arrived from Rome—he is a man of seventy years who worked on the original drainage of the plain and he has offered to give us a hand. We went all over the problem of the site and he will start work with us tomorrow attempting to construct the pit of planks and poles at the bottom of the hole to hold back the sand—a kind of caisson for the sump where we place the pumps. There is sure a hell of a lot of water. We should be ready to uncover the ruins by the fifteenth and I will phone you just as soon as we can see anything. Keep your fingers crossed."

Again we were to wait in vain for the call that was to tell us that the five years of work had finally succeeded and that Sybaris had been found. A week later he wrote, "Our engineer, Garrone, has left, but Beth Ralph and Enrico are on the job and I will take over as my own engineer! It is tough, the sand pours into the sump about as fast as we dig it out, gained only one foot during the past week—and as usual our problem is pumps. The generator will not pull all four pumps as we had hoped and Beth is off to Taranto to see if she can get another generator—if so we will buy another electric pump and put five to work. The gasoline pumps ruin us. Just as we get the water down so we can dig, they plug up and the whole thing floods again. The electric pumps are wonderful but the ones we have are not enough for the flow. There are four or five sorgenti like great fountains. We can now see clearly masses of roof tiles and blocks of stone occasionally above water, so we are right on top of the ruins, whatever they are. In the sump we are shoveling out masses of broken tiles, many of them burned, and some pottery, all of them sixth century B.C. I am now hoping to get it all cleared by the twentieth. Why not come out before the twenty-fifth on the chance that there will be something to see? At least you can see the remains of buildings occupied before the fall of Sybaris."

On the sixteenth I received a wire from Fro, "Pumps worked. Found archaic building all burned. Only roof tiles and sherds. Not worth seeing. You may be right. Will finish this week." By this time we were becoming accustomed to disappointments and almost began to feel that the finding of Sybaris would be an anticlimax. The reference "You may be right" was to the fact that Susy and I had felt, from the finding of the first archaic pottery at the long wall, that Sybaris must lie inland, the pottery having been washed down the stream. By nature I have always been impatient and have never learned the discipline of the scientist who can pursue his research for years on end, but I was finding by experience that infinite patience and continually sticking at it might eventually bring the results we were seeking. Although we were disappointed, we were also elated, for this was the first structure of the time of Sybaris to be found on the plain.

The excavation had been about fifty feet long and thirty feet wide with an enormous amount of sand and water pressure. About fifteen feet below the surface rough walls and quantities of roof tiles were found. All the material, including sherds, had been burned. Only one large block of cut stone was found and the corners of two buildings. All the material, however, was of the sixth century B.C. Fro leaned more than ever to the theory that this was only the port, just as the neighboring city of Metapontum had a port which was separated from the city. It was now necessary to wait until the new magnetometer was ready, which would not be until August at the earliest. The new instrument would be used in this same area, not only to test its accuracy in comparison with what was already known, but also to see whether there might be buildings located at a greater depth which this magnetometer would disclose on account of its ability to penetrate the soil more deeply. Although the Italian archaeologists were quite positive that this was Sybaris, Fro refused to make any announcement and would only state that it might be the great city. Before doing any further excavation, which would have to be undertaken on a much more elaborate scale in order not to disturb the archaic walls which were believed to lie in this area, it would be necessary to try to locate additional structures below the surface with the magnetometer.

The new instrument was ready for testing on the fifteenth of August, and Beth went to Arizona, where the tests were carried out by the technical staff of Varian Associates. A few changes had to be made after the first trials, the most serious defect being the machine's sensitivity to temperature. It would not be until some time in September that it would be ready for use in Italy.

We arranged to meet Fro and Beth at Sybaris on the seventh of October and spend some time there, as the final discovery seemed so close. On the fourth we had spent the day at Paestum, planning to go the next day to Herculaneum, but we received a telephone call that evening from Fro, who had reached Sybaris earlier than planned. He asked us to meet him the following day, so much to our regret we have not yet been to the great city which was buried so deeply by Vesuvius at the beginning of the Christian era. Beth and Fro were at the hotel when we arrived, after what we felt was an ample day's trip, but their hospitality, vigor, and enthusiasm were such that they insisted on our climbing into the Volkswagen station wagon for a forty-mile trip to dinner at Bagamoyo. It was a good dinner at a lovely spot on the beach, looking out over the still waters of the Ionian Sea, and over a bottle of wine we were brought up to date on all that had been happening. Apparently the new magnetometer was a superb success and was picking up anomalies far in excess and at greater depths than had been shown on any of the former instruments. In fact, there were sufficient readings to allow the presumption that there might be a whole city lying at a depth of about twenty feet, and within a one-mile radius of the long wall. This could be large enough for Sybaris, so we went to bed that night with the happy feeling that perhaps the end was now in sight.

On the morning of the eighth of October, Susy, Fro, and I started with a walk over the hill of Torre del Mordillo, where we found countless additional sherds lying on top of the recently plowed soil. All of them, however, were later than the time of Sybaris, but were largely Greek with a few later Roman remains. We went from there to the spring of Fonte del Fico. On the road we heard a car behind us blowing its horn, and turned to see Beth in the station wagon with one of the men who operates the magnetometer. She jumped out waving a large map at us and, as she approached, called out, "We have found it. We have Sybaris!" You can imagine the excitement. The historic moment hoped for for more than a hundred years had finally arrived, and the secrets of twenty-five hundred years were about to be uncovered. A map showing all the readings of the new magnetometer plotted in their exact location was quickly spread on the trunk compartment. Beth had spent a large part of the night in working over the map and had not only shown all the readings, but had also plotted in the lines of the buildings below the surface. These plainly showed a large number of structures, one of them being over one hundred feet long and facing due east and west, which was exactly the way the Greeks sited their temples. We surely had a city and thought we could even see from the readings where a gate in the walls had been. We hailed her as the discoverer of Sybaris, a prize in archaeology which might prove to be second only to the finding of King Tutankhamen's tomb in 1922 by Howard Carter after six years of effort. We immediately followed her to the site where the men were working with the *spillo* and were constantly striking tiles or stones at a level of about nineteen feet below the surface. In an adjoining field Beth went to work with her magnetometer, which was giving frequent and excellent readings of stone structures. It was all extremely exciting because there could be no doubt that a city of some kind lay beneath these peaceful pastures, a city of some twenty-five hundred years ago where men had lived and worked, enjoyed ease and fought battles, and developed a culture which we hoped would be revealed to us when we were able to penetrate the clay, the sand, and the water.

One of the men went back to Sybaris for the fresh-baked bread which was an essential of the midday meal, and we all stretched out in the shade of a hedgerow in the midst of a herd of cattle. Every now and then one of the cows would become too curious and would have to be chased away from the water and wine bottles, only to return again in a few minutes. It was a perfect fall day, warm enough to sit in the sun with pleasure, with puffy white clouds floating over the mountains in the background. We were fortunate in having with us one of Italy's foremost archaeological experts on archaic ruins. Everyone was extremely joyful over the results, which far exceeded anything to date and gave full promise of solving the riddle which we had been working on for so long. Dottoressa Zancani, the Italian archaeologist, said to Susy and me that Fro should announce the finding of Sybaris before the news leaked out, as there could be no shadow of doubt that this was Sybaris. What further proof was needed? Archaic sherds and roof tiles at the proper level and outlines

*Fro, Beth, and I: We Have Found Sybaris!*

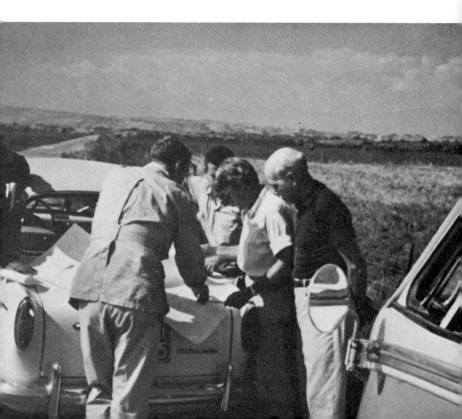

of a city showing beneath the soil. Fro was not prepared to say that the city had been found until he could actually see the foundations of the buildings and, he hoped, the bases of some of the columns. By this time we had given up hope that any standing temples similar to those at Paestum would be unearthed.

It was agreed that it was now too late in the year to begin a major excavation, and anything less than a well-planned engineering study for the elimination of the water before digging would entail the risk of a cave-in and the damaging of the walls of the archaic structures. It was decided to continue work with the magnetometer and the *spillo* in order to outline the size of the city and to determine what large buildings, streets, and city walls might be hidden. The buildings of the city were followed for almost one-half mile before work was stopped. All of this would provide essential data for deciding on the exact location of the excavation to be made in late April of the following year. The summer's work came to a dramatic conclusion early in November when a cow kicked over the sensor which was fixed in the ground and put it more or less permanently out of use. At any rate, it was decided, in the good old Sybaritic Greek fashion, that this was a warning from the gods that if we continued, success would not crown our efforts. With befitting vinous oblations to propitiate the gods, we packed the instruments in the Volkswagen, and another summer was ended, but this year it was with a feeling of certainty and confidence which we had never had before.

During the winter months we sought advice on the best method of getting rid of the problem of the flooding of the excavation. Raikes had already suggested the well-point system, and now Dr. Meyerhoff informed us of a method of using a caisson type of retaining wall, which would permit the drying up of the pit and at the same time prevent the collapse of the side wall.

It was also possible to try a clay called bentonite which has a unique molecular construction whereby it absorbs an enormous quantity of water and swells up during the process. It is dug in open pits and then finally granulated before being sold commercially. While it is used largely in the construction of dams for stopping any leakage, we investigated the question of using it at Sybaris by digging a deep trench all around the hole to be excavated and then putting the bentonite into this trench. Another possibility was the use of a chemical which would be introduced into the soil to any desired depth around the pit. When the chemical dried out, it would harden the soil to about the consistency of a soft sandstone and thereby prevent any water from entering the excavation. We would still have the water rising from the floor, but there would be no further seepage from the sides or the constant trouble and real danger from cave-ins. This chemical, made by one of the largest companies in the United States, seemed to us to be the best approach to the problem. But the cost of this method would be far greater than our modest budget could provide, and also we were not very confident of our success with a possibly inexperienced foreign contracting company doing the work. Through mutual friends we approached the management of the American company, and Fro and I were invited to their offices for lunch. We explained our problem and asked them if they would supply the material and the technical supervision for the treatment of an excavation of about one hundred feet square; we hoped thereby to uncover an area large enough to show us the "temple." We stressed the importance of this completely new method of archaeology and the possible value to their company of the publicity they would obtain from a participation in the discovery of Sybaris. They were not particularly impressed by this argument, so we sought their aid in the form of a charitable contribution to the Museum as an educational institution. We were not very good salesmen, for both these pleas fell on fallow ground. We could not have received a more cordial reception and polite refusal or a better lunch. In fact, it was so good that Fro slept for over an hour on the way home in the car. We were deeply disappointed by our failure, for it was not so much their financial support that we sought, although this was important to us, but their technical and managerial ability we believed would have assured our success.

Meanwhile, the sherds had arrived for study at the Museum, and one disturbing bit of evidence appeared. Tiny pieces of what seemed to be mortar had turned up in the rubble. This mortar probably would not have been used by the Greeks at this time and gave a warning that any pronouncements on what lay deep below the surface should surely be withheld until after an actual examination of the temple.

# XVIII

# ANTICLIMAX
# 1966

B y March it had almost been determined that the most practical method was the well-point system around a much smaller hole, approximately thirty feet square. Mr. Raikes was asked to join the expedition in April. He was fortunately available at this time, and wrote: "As you know, I have been firmly convinced that you were hell-bent on suicide/homicide digging in the way that you were, from the time you first came to see me in Rome! So count me in."

Beth Ralph was back in Sybaris in March and was planning the next steps with Raikes. Fro would be in Rome on April 5 and have time to consult with Raikes before going to Libya. While awaiting Rainey's arrival in Sybaris later in April, Beth was to work with the magnetometer further inland and south of the Crati, especially as Fro was still not convinced that the Parco del Cavallo—Lattughella area was where Sybaris lay. When they met in Rome, they discussed drilling one well at the site abandoned in the fall which had been so full of promise, to a depth of forty-five feet, putting one large pump in this to draw out the water, then digging a hole ten feet square and shoring up the sides with boards. They believed this was comparatively inexpensive and would prove whether the "temple" shown by the magnetometer the previous fall was Roman or Hellenic or archaic. If one of the former two, not much time was lost, and if it was really a Greek building of the time of Sybaris, then a large excavation could prove well worth-while. When I received his letter, I was really frightened, for it seemed to me more suicidal/homicidal than anything that had been done yet. I pictured someone—probably Fro—at the bottom of a hole ten feet wide and twenty feet deep when the shoring gave way and the sides collapsed on him. I wrote him immediately of my fears and said that Dr. Meyerhoff was also worried and felt it very unsafe and had told me to put the fear of God into him not to do it. I suggested that a pit at least fifty feet square be dug and that a caisson be sunk for the last eight feet. Fortunately, when Rainey arrived at Sybaris on the twenty-sixth of April, he found that no equipment was available to excavate in the way that they had discussed.

They decided on the well-point system, making the dig about thirty-three feet square. Contracts were entered into with a company to do the well-point drilling and installation. The faithful Spina with his large power shovel was to excavate the dirt down to a level from which hand-digging could be done as soon as buildings were encountered. The contract called for completion of the work in twelve days, but as usual unexpected difficulties arose in getting the well-points to penetrate the hard sand. In any case, what was now being done was entirely safe from the point of view of working in the mud. By the twenty-eighth all thirty-six well-points had been put down around the perimeter of the hole and the one big pump was ready to start its work collecting the water from all

*Well-Point Drainage*

thirty-six well-points. The first structure was hit at twelve feet below the surface, and from this point on the digging was to be done by hand.

When the digging started, it was found the building was badly destroyed and the walls were all of very poor construction, made of bricks, mortar, and boulders. All late Roman and all the sherds were Roman. The walls were buried in masses of rubble from some fallen building, but everything was late Roman. The sides of the pit began to collapse into the cut, and cables had to be rigged to keep the well-points from sliding into the hole. At this point the only hope was that the early Greek structures might lie below the Roman ruins, but the prospect was indeed a gloomy one.

We had arranged that Fro would telephone us as soon as he was sure he had found the city (and after all that the other experts had said, we felt more than half convinced that it was Sybaris), and Susy and I would come over the next day to unearth some of the marvelous works of art we were to find in the temple.

Having heard nothing from him by May 7, and knowing that the work was finished the night before, I realized that our hopes had been unfulfilled again; but I wanted news badly, so I telephoned to Sybaris only to find that Fro had left. I finally traced him to Mr. Delmege's apartment in Rome, where I hoped he was drowning his sorrow. The conversation went something like this: O.H.B.: "Fro, I'm sorry you didn't have any luck." F.G.R.: "Orville, it was the most glorious, complete and unmitigated failure. Every damn thing was late Roman and not worth looking at." O.H.B.: "Did you find any pottery or lamps or anything worth seeing?" F.G.R.: "Absolutely nothing worth even picking up. But [and here the scientist got the better of his disappointment] the magnetometer was a marvelous success. The buildings were all there exactly in the location where it showed them to be. We now have conclusive proof of the value of the instrument in archaeology." We discussed future plans. Beth had gone to Helice in Greece at the request of the Greek Government and would be away for ten days, when Fro would join her at Sybaris for the next step. She had left one magnetometer at Sybaris, and two graduate students were to be there to operate it, so that later in the summer we would have both machines working in the plain; hopefully on my part, further inland, and also south of the Crati, where at that time I thought Sybaris might lie.

His letter to me is of interest as a firsthand account of the results of five years of work! "It is really surprising to find that the late Roman structure went right down into the sand at nineteen feet. Not a damn thing under it! I expected some archaic sherds at least. We had a hell of a time with water as usual, but when Enrico [Mueller] got back from Rome and put the fear of God into his workers they stuck at it in the mud until we got down to the sand and the bottom of the wall—then that was the maximum effective depth of the well-points and the sorgente hit us again.

"The instruments worked fine! It was a massive building just where the magnetometer put it—but unfortunately they can't tell us what period! Spina is now filling in the hole—and Signora Zancani had rushed down here from Sorrento at my urgent request to expertise on the Greek structure. My wire did not reach her in time and I have put her to a lot of trouble for nothing. Foti was here to see the hole at the maximum depth. He is also very depressed and very cooperative. President Saragat made a nice speech yesterday on the radio about our work on the Sybaris plain. He has just been down here.

"No, I don't really know what to do. First go to Rome to unscramble a hold-up on the aerial photography and then return to meet Beth to decide where we survey next. I think north and west because that is where we have found archaic structures without Roman on top. Also more exploration south and inland. Have you any ideas? Do let me know what you think. Anyway the plain is beautiful this time of year—on top—just very ugly when you get under the surface."

I thought this a fine letter, and it shows the character of the man who was to find Sybaris. There is no note of self-pity for all the years of work and thought which he had given to the search, and he ends with the idea of going ahead, staying at Sybaris and continuing with the instruments and drills in new areas.

In spite of the disappointment, Beth was back again with the magnetometer, working to the north of the excavation where only archaic sherds had been found, and all in a living level. Her purpose was to outline the size of the area in order to determine if it was large enough to be a city. Many anomalies were shown, and the area would be drilled to determine how far north the archaic remains lie. By the first week in June Varian Associates had sent over another magnetometer, and along with it came two enthusiastic young geophysicists who had been trained at the Varian factory in the use of the instrument. This doubled the amount of territory which could be covered, and the presence of the young men gave new life to those who had been working so long.

In July, Fro wrote me his conclusions from the work done during the summer. He said, "I am thoroughly convinced that we have discovered the port of Sybaris as well as the port of Thurii and Thurii-Copiae. With the cesium magnetometer during June, 1966, we were able to circumscribe the archaic Greek settlement just north of the Stombi road where it joins the Bruscate road. This is an area measuring about one kilometer east and west and a little over one-half kilometer north and south. The test excavation there last year exposed the only archaic structure so far discovered on the plain of Sybaris. Our drills indicated that this small area has an archaic living level between four and five meters deep. There are no late Greek and Roman ruins superimposed over it. But with all of our drill holes there, and all the instrument surveys in this area, we have located no extensive buildings or ruins of temples or other public buildings such as those found at Metapontum, Locri, Paestum, etc. The limited size of this settlement and the absence of any large structures lead me to the conclusion that this is the ancient port of Sybaris which lay very close to the ancient shoreline and probably on the bank of a river, either the Sybaris or the Crati.

"Between the long wall and the present bed of the Crati, there are a great many structures lying anywhere from three to six meters deep, which I believe to be all late Greek or Roman. In any case, in six excavations carried on over the years in this area, we have found only late Greek and Roman structures with sherds from the early archaic Greek period in the sands below the late Greek and Roman ruins. Therefore, I assume that this area, south of the long wall, is the site of the late Greek and Roman ports. In other words, after the destruction of Sybaris, the port area was moved about one kilometer to the south. We know from the clay deposits packed in around the late Greek and Roman walls that this region, during the late Greek and Roman times, was repeatedly a lagoon in which the fine clay silts were deposited. If I am right in concluding that we have located the ports, then where is Sybaris?

"The famous ruins at Le Muraglie and at the Fonte del Fico are all Roman. The aqueduct coming from Fonte del Fico down to the Parco del Cavallo area is also Roman. There were, however, five or six late Greek burial mounds in the Fonte del Fico region. Otherwise, most of the known Greek sites seem to concentrate in the northern part rather than the southern part of the plain of the Crati. For example, there is the well-known Greek site at Francavilla which was contemporary with Sybaris, and late Greek sites near Doria and at Casa Chidichimo. There is also the late Greek site at Torre Mordillo. From this I suspect that the actual site of Sybaris itself must lie somewhere in the northern part of the plain or on terraces over the plain. There is a further indication of this in the surviving place names. For example, Buffaloria, near Sybaris station, and Doria.

"During the month of July, two crews with four cesium magnetometers are running long lines or grids across the whole plain. Nothing so far has turned up. The new aerial photographs will be ready for study in September or October and I am hoping they will turn up something either on the plain inland from Parco del Cavallo, or up on the terraces just north of the plain. I must conclude with caution that the Parco del Cavallo area may indeed be the site of Sybaris itself, but this seems to be unlikely since with all our drilling and instrument surveys we cannot find massive constructions which are certain to be associated with the city of Sybaris."

We were now at a standstill, and the winter of 1966 was one of gloom and depression. What to do next? I was fearful that any day might bring a phone call from Fro saying he had spent too much of his time away from the work of the Museum and that he saw no useful purpose which would be served by going on for another year. We had not received the aerial photographs, and we had no definite ideas as to where the work should begin in the spring. With what had been done by the magnetometer and the literally thousands of drill holes, all we had definitely found was the port of Sybaris, but no indication of where we might locate the city itself. Some photographs arrived in December, and there were a few hazy lines that might be the outline of walls, but nothing of any magnitude. It would be easy in the spring to prove whether these marks were actual walls or only variations in the topography. They might even prove to be ancient drainage ditches. However, there was one hope. These photographs had all been taken at high altitudes, and the ones which showed anything abnormal had all been made with a camera using infrared film. We at once decided to engage a helicopter to take infrared pictures at low altitude and to endeavor to have this done in May as soon after the harvest as possible. Beth could be there at the time to direct the work. Before she left in May, 1967, we met with Fro at the Museum, and I heard for the first time some news which, to me, was exciting. Per-

haps I was only looking for encouragement and was willing to
follow any new lead. Between four and five miles north of
where we had been working along the Crati, there is another
river, the Raganello. In these days this former great river dries
up in summer and is considered a *torrente* by the Italians.
Bearing in mind that we do not know which was the ancient
Sybaris River, I could easily persuade myself that it could
have been the Raganello. The city of Sybaris could lie between it and the Crati and would be in a hollow.

I argued that we, and all previous expeditions, had been
mistaken in accepting the present-day Coscile as the ancient
Sybaris River. If the Raganello was the original Sybaris River,
then we should move farther north in our search, as the city
would still lie between two rivers. This was a brand-new
theory, as no former archaeologist had ever mentioned this
river, nor is there any record of exploratory work having been
done near it. Again I was to be proved wrong.

Signora Paolo Zancani Montuoro had shown Susy and
me some ninth- and eighth-century graves which she had excavated in the foothills a short distance from where they rose
from the plain and were bordered by the Raganello. These
graves were of the crudest possible form, being little more
than pits which were lined with stones picked up on the hillside, but in these graves were artifacts undoubtedly of this
early period. She had also found the ruins of a small early
temple and, most important of all, a bronze plaque. On this
tablet, in archaic Greek of the sixth century, was an inscrip-
tion telling how a young man from the Sybaris plain had won
an event at the Olympic games and then, in carrying out his
vow, had dedicated the tablet of Athena. Here finally was our
first direct reference to Sybaris by a Sybarite, and we had
Pausanius's statement that Philytas had won the boxing at
Olympia. Equally if not more important, Signora Zancani

had found several graves containing well-preserved archaic pottery of the time of Sybaris. As the Greeks, with the exception of the Spartans, buried their dead outside the city walls, it seemed to me that at last we might find the answer as to why this huge city had kept its secret for so long. I argued that we, and all past seekers, by accepting the present Coscile as the Sybaris River, had been misled in interpreting the ancient accounts and that the ancient Sybaris River was actually the Raganello.

Whether you call it keeping an open mind, foolish optimism, or the counsel of despair, it did not take us long to decide that Beth should begin her work with the magnetometer and a drill between the Raganello and the archaic graves on the foothills. We also had the additional hope that the new infrared pictures might show us something of value.

Shortly after starting work along the Raganello, Beth found anomalies which gave us hope, but when the drills were put to work, they only proved to be part of an ancient road, and no potsherds were found.

In May, Signor Adamasteanu, the Superintendent of Antiquities for Apulia, was able to have pictures taken of the Sybaris plain, using our infrared film, and of the neighboring Greek city of Siris in which he was interested. Our usual luck continued when we received a telegram after the film had been developed. It read, "No photos Sybaris area camera shutter stuck stop. Good results for Siris—letter follows." The letter was enthusiastic about what had been shown for Siris, so we were still able to feel optimistic about what we might see in pictures of our plain. Again the grapes were just out of our reach, but they still might be sweet when we plucked them, so we asked for an immediate retaking of the aerial photography. The finished prints were now promised to us for the seventeenth of July, and Fro wired Beth that he and I would arrive on the sixteenth.

Leaving the Raganello, Beth began work at the western end of the long wall. The reader will recall that this huge structure lay north of the Crati and was in the shape of a dogleg with the angle pointing north. Exciting news came quickly. The magnetometer picked up strong anomalies making a right angle at its western end and running in a southerly direction. The anomalies were so good that rapid progress was made, and they were even found in the bed of the river, running south for over half a mile. Beth immediately set to work with the drill and the *spillo* to prove her findings. Thrilling results ensued. The wall was struck at a uniform depth of fifteen feet and was apparently of quite different construction from that of the long wall. It had a width of between twelve and fifteen feet and could have been a city wall for defense, in comparison to the narrow width of the long wall. Numerous sherds came up in the drill with the concentration largely to the western side of the wall, which would logically place them inside the city away from the sea. North of the Crati there was again considerable Roman pottery, but south of it nothing but Greek sherds appeared, including one fine black piece with a handle. However, the pottery was probably all fifth-century and too late for Sybaris. Beth was anxious to excavate at once and was arranging for Spina and his power shovel to come to the job. We persuaded her, however, to continue with the drill and magnetometer to try to prove that it was of the time of Sybaris. We already had ample proof of late Greek and Roman occupation, so we curbed our mounting enthusiasm and continued the probing. It was fortunate we did so, for our realization was to lie elsewhere.

The airplane pictures had finally arrived. However, they

were a bitter disappointment, as the experts could find no signs of a hidden city. Shortly after we received them, a photo-geologist arrived at the Museum saying he had heard of the pictures and would like to examine them. As he had excellent references from two large oil companies, we were delighted to have his help. Within a few days he returned with a complete map of the ancient city which he had interpreted from the photographs. According to him, it lay about fifteen hundred feet north of the long wall and the city walls had a circumference of about six miles, which would agree with ancient descriptions of Sybaris. The eastern wall ran due north, almost to the coast line, then turned westwart to a point .6 mile from the present Sybaris railroad station. It was in the center of this area that we had found our only sixth-century building, which was too small to make any judgment as to whether it was part of a great city. We needed a temple or some major structure to say definitely that Sybaris had been found. Several other outlines which he claimed he saw in the photographs led us to believe that this might be our site. He plotted on his map the old beds of the Crati and Sybaris Rivers, and they conformed to the ancient accounts in that they flowed to the sea on either side of the city. In addition, he saw traces of an ancient stream bed which ran through the city, thus apparently confirming Strabo's account that the Crotoniates had diverted the river over the city when they conquered it.

What to do now? After much discussion we sent him back to Italy to try to prove what he had seen in the photographs by an intensive drilling campaign, with particular reference to outlining the city walls and locating some large structure, such as a temple.

After a considerable amount of drilling the geologist reported that the drill being used was an improper one and very destructive. He was not able to find any large buildings or blocks of stone in the walls where the photographs presumably showed them. He explained this by saying that the drill went through stone, but Dr. Rainey's experience and mine had been that the drill would not penetrate any stone structure. He found archaeological material in thirty-six of thirty-seven holes drilled, but not necessarily archaic. His drilling showed material to the north, near the present railroad station, and also that this area was dry to a depth of twelve feet. His report concluded with the recommendation that further infrared air pictures be made as soon as the fields became green in the spring.

We were deeply disappointed with these results, as our hopes had been raised by the map he had given us, made from his readings of the aerial pictures. Others had been unable to see any outline of walls on the photographs, so we were delighted with his findings and desired to have proof of them. However, no tangible evidence had been produced, and it was now too late to continue any work in the plain, as the rains had started.

# XIX

# FINALE

In spite of the fact that so little was accomplished in 1967, I felt strangely happy and optimistic during the winter, but I realized that Fro was entirely right in not wanting to announce any discovery until he could be sure there were some large structures under the land where we now thought Sybaris lay. We had plenty of indications that we had been walking over the site of the city every day, the cesium magnetometer had proved itself and we had found many anomalies with it, the drills had brought up countless archaic sherds, and all in all I had a feeling that this was it. I had no archaeological reputation to lose, nor would anything I said carry any weight with the scientific world, so I wanted to announce the discovery, but I waited in impatience and tried to think of anything that might be of help for the coming spring.

I am sure I bothered Fro a lot during the winter; he was always such fun to talk with. Imagine how any scholar must feel to have a rank and inexperienced amateur who is always making suggestions as to how he should carry out his life's

# PROBABLE SITE OF SYBARIS
### Entire area intensively drilled and surveyed by magnetometer

▬▬▬ Possible limits of city ✖ Excavations

METERS
0    400    800

PROBABLE BED OF ANCIENT SYBARIS RIVER

Area of
1968 drilling ✖

STOMBI ROAD

BRUSCATE ROAD

Casa Bianca

Lattughella

LONG WALL

PARCO
DEL
CAVALLO

CRATI RIVER

AQUEDUCT

PROBABLE BED OF ANCIENT CRATI RIVER

RAILROAD

N

IONIAN SEA ⟶

work, about which he knows so much. No matter how sure I felt of the location, I did not want to leave any other possibility unexplored, and in January of 1968 I was writing Fro asking for an intensive study of the infrared photographs, new pictures to be taken of the probable site and going further south and west. The same letter urged that we test a new drill in this country, buy a core drill (this would bring to the surface a solid column of earth showing the exact condition of the soil, living levels, and location of pottery sherds in the soil removed), and drill for tombs in the so-called Cavallari area deeper than he had gone down. I hoped if we found tombs south of the Crati and north by the railroad station, we could count on the city's lying between them, remembering that the Greeks buried their dead outside the city. Other suggestions were to drill to the west of Torre Della Chiesa and at Masseria Chidichimo, also south of the Crati and west of the new wall where Beth had found nothing but archaic sherds. Finally I asked him to excavate the northern limits near the railroad station. When I read this now, I realize I was asking him to send two or three expeditions and to spend all his time there supervising the work. Strangely enough, he did not laugh at me for such large ideas but agreed to set about immediately finding a new drill and testing it out. Beth, however, wrote me a well-deserved and hot letter saying, "Your letter to Fro of January 22 has just come to my attention, and quite frankly, I am appalled by your suggestion." She went on to say, "With this new magnetometer, I am willing to guarantee that if a buried structure exists on the plain of Sybaris, it can be detected. What is more, it can be detected even if the sensor of the magnetometer is five meters (over 15 feet) away laterally on the surface." I think this sentence shows, more than anything else, what enormous strides in the development of the instrument Varian Associates and Beth

had made in the five years since she began using the first proton magnetometer, which could be accurate only at the depth
of a few feet. Now twenty feet underground was easy for her.
Even if we had not found Sybaris, an enormous contribution
had been made to the science of archaeology and future expeditions would have their work vastly simplified. In May, 1968,
she went to Elis in Greece, about seventy miles from Olympia,
and within a few days had picked up a buried city. She was
so immediately successful that the Greeks were able to uncover the ruins as she proceeded ahead of them with the magnetometer. What a change from the old methods of painstaking digging and searching! It made me green with envy
when she showed me the pictures of the excavations, with
the walls of houses standing intact and no water to cope with.
However, even though the magnetometer was showing structures all over our site, we had to find a way to prove they were
there, and the only way to do it was to drill before we started
to dig. How futile it would be to excavate with a steam shovel
an enormous pit, with five huge pumps going twenty-four
hours a day, and then only find some loose stones at the
bottom.

We spent a great deal of time in the winter of 1967 discussing just what to do and finally agreed that it was important to have more infrared pictures of the plain and that in
the spring we should begin intensive drilling. Fro approached
the Italian authorities about the photographs, and they very
generously offered to make them for us at their expense. We
owe them a debt of gratitude for this gesture of assistance
and for their permission to make the pictures.

Our old drill, after so many years, was wearing out and
also it was exasperatingly slow, with many breakdowns. It
would seem that it would be a comparatively easy matter to
find a good light drill. We wanted one that could be mounted

on the back of a jeep so that it would be able to be moved easily from place to place in the fields. We were able to do only about eight or ten holes a day because after drilling a hole the only way we could remove the bit was to set up a tripod above it and with a series of pulleys pull it out by hand. This all took a great deal of time. I consulted a large contracting firm accustomed to drilling foundations, and I also went to a nationally known engineering company. Neither of them could be of any help as all their machinery was much heavier and more expensive than we needed. As the telephone company is so persistent in its advertising of letting the yellow pages find it for you, I turned to them and after a few calls found in Indiana exactly what we were looking for. Fro and Beth had a demonstration and reported it would do our job beautifully. We were lucky in that the company had an agent in Italy, and we arranged for the drill to be at Sybaris the first of May when we would be able to get in the fields.

Having found a drill, Fro was off to Rome in March. Through the good offices of Mr. Russell Harris and Dr. Enzo Mazzaglia, of the American Embassy, he was able to arrange a meeting with Dr. Giuseppe Donato, director of the Government Center for Archaeological Research and Documentation. Dr. Donato was extremely helpful and cooperative and worked directly with General Bacich of the Air Force. It was agreed the Italian Air Force would make the photographs at once. Fro went to Sybaris to be on hand when the plane took off, but for several days the weather was not good enough to photograph. He had taken with him an outstanding young American archaeologist, Mrs. Edward C. Carter, who was living in Rome where her husband was teaching.

As she had directed digs for the Museum in Iraq, Libya, and Italy, Fro had complete confidence in her ability, which she quickly proved. Mrs. Carter holds her Ph.D. from Bryn Mawr and is a Research Associate at the Museum.

While at Sybaris Fro met a group which was taking one of the interesting University Museum tours of ancient sites and showed them the various ruined cities on the plain, ending with a lunch which unfortunately almost poisoned most of them. As Fro described it, "all that dried pork sausage was enough to sink a Marine." He went on to Greece to return to Sybaris when the drill arrived, which was not until later in May, the air photos having been completed in early April.

By the first of June, Mrs. Carter was actively at work with Domenico and Giuseppe Falcone operating the drill and Bruno Frascino, a young man with training in chemistry, to act as superintendent and accurately map the location of any results. The type of difficulty in reaching the fields is well explained by a comment in Mrs. Carter's letter, "the passage is adequately barred with two chains and six padlocks. The man with the keys lives in Cosenza and has left the keys with a man in Cassano who has gone to Taranto! Perhaps we shall get in next week." Another difficulty arose for her as the Police Marshal of Trebisacce insisted that she leave her hotel, as it was the local center of vice. In the beginning she drilled to a depth of forty-five feet and even as much as sixty feet, but later on, as we began striking the Sybaris living level and archaic sherds at fifteen feet, we rarely went below twenty feet. As the drill is removed from the ground, there are several feet of soil tightly packed around the spirals; below this there is a bluish gray clay of the consistency of very heavy putty, all of it soaking wet. Below the clay will come more soil, and it was in this soil that we were finding the Sybaris pottery and brick sherds, all at a practically uniform depth of fifteen feet. The packed dirt from around the drill is peeled off with great care, broken apart, and searched for any sherds.

By the middle of June, Mrs. Carter was able to report that she was carefully tracing the outline of the cultural zone (limits of the occupied area of the city) and that she had possibly found the south bank of the bed of the ancient Sybaris River. This was of the greatest interest, for if the old bed of this river was north of the area in which all the archaic sherds lay, we could confirm the ancient accounts that the city lay between two rivers. We would, presumably, have found the northern limits of Sybaris. She was also anxious to find the former bed of the southern river, the Crati, but this was difficult because of the construction of a new road.

The air pictures were finished the middle of June, and Fro saw them in Rome. They had taken twelve hundred photographs and had printed them nine by nine inches. They were all excellent, but it was not until three months later that we were able to obtain our copies, and by then they were useful only to confirm our magnetometer findings. He was actively occupied with the drilling and wrote me that the area in which they were working looked more and more as if it was big enough for Sybaris. All the sherds he was getting at the fifteen-foot depth were archaic and, of course, Sybaris was the only city in the plain at that time; however, he had still found no large structures and only one small wall.

On June 27, I received a telegram from Mrs. Carter saying, "Perhaps have located other river." I promptly telephoned her in Rome where she had gone to join her husband, for they both had to go on to Greece, and she would be unable to return to Sybaris until possibly late fall. She told me she was very happy with the results as she felt she had found the old bed of the Crati and we therefore had the north and south limits of the city. The distance north and south, she said, was approximately four kilometers and east and west would appear to be close to two kilometers. This corresponded roughly with the figures given by Strabo and would possibly be larger than Athens of that day. In her mind there was no question but that we had finally succeeded.

Coming from an archaeologist with her reputation, this was marvelous news, and it only remained to strike some large building in order that we could excavate. Now, at the end of eight years, here was success. It all seemed unbelievable, as at many times during those years we could not help feeling that we had set ourselves a hopeless task. There was, and is, still much to be done, but I felt that finally the discovery of this almost mythological city, which had been searched for by so many archaeologists from different countries for so long a time, could be announced .

When she left, Bruno was placed in charge to continue a systematic plan of drilling laid out by Dr. Rainey. It was no longer necessary to have a trained archaeologist on the spot as all the sherds were archaic at the Sybaris level and we were looking only for walls and indications of large buildings. One success followed another, and two days later I received a wire from Fro saying, "Discovered structure 28 meters long in archaic zone." We had it! It might even be a temple, for the beautiful Theseion in Athens, one of the best preserved of all temples, is about thirty-two meters, and the Temple of Demeter of Agrigentum was twenty-seven meters. There were many roof tiles along the walls of this new building which the drill pierced, and the lowest foot of the drill was packed with bits of tile when it was withdrawn. The walls were hit by the drill nearer the surface than the Sybaris level and therefore propounded two questions. Could it be that we had a structure where the walls were still standing? Or had we struck a small temple built above an older building? Digging alone would tell.

Before leaving Sybaris for Cyprus, Fro had also checked the southern limits of the city south of the Crati. He found three levels of occupation: Roman, late Greek, and then again our archaic level at the bottom. The occupation ended about a kilometer south of the present river, and he felt that we now had both old river beds plotted. At that time of year the heat is so intense that the working day started at five and ended at one. It was also difficult work because the new building had been found in a field of brush and brambles. I checked with a contracting firm on the probable cost of sinking a caisson around this newly found building and was blandly told that it could be done for around $100,000. A later telephone call from Fro told me that he finally thought that we had found Sybaris but that he still would like to find a larger building for complete proof before making any announcement, and even if he did not strike such a structure he would be willing, at the end of the summer, to write a scientific account of the work and end with the conclusion that Sybaris had been found. He had outlined the size of the city, had found nothing but archaic sherds in this area at the fifteen- to twenty-foot level below present grade, and had hit numerous structures with the drill. As other archaeologists said, "What further proof do you want?"

On the twelfth of July, Bruno reported that his drill had struck another building and had brought up masses of pottery, brick, and bones. He asked for instructions about digging so that he could ask the farmer not to cultivate the field. How kind they all were to us. However, we decided to continue drilling and finding more buildings. This proved wise because by early August Bruno had found a new structure and reported three columns and a wall in a line extending east and west. A temple? A human tooth seemed to clinch the argument that we were working in a living level! There was talk of the Italian Government's wishing to try to drain the site so that digging would be made easier, but this would have to come later. We now had several buildings, and a letter from Mrs. Carter had an amusing sentence to my lay mind, "If the drilling is continued in a close and methodical pattern, one should be able to produce a reasonably accurate plan of downtown Sybaris in a matter of months." I had never quite thought of Sybaris in terms of a downtown business district!

In September, Susy and I met Fro in Rome, and our sister-in-law, Mrs. John H. W. Ingersoll, who had been to Sybaris twice, was with us. She was a great addition, not only being a lovely person with an amazing knowledge of Italian art and architecture, but also an excellent chauffeur who spoke fluent Italian in comparison with Fro's and my halting efforts. Our first step was to try to get the infrared photographs, still in the possession of the Government. We met with General Bacich and Professor Donato. The photographs were promised for our return to Rome, and I was able to bring home the ones of the particular area in which we were working. The remaining huge bundle was shipped back to the Museum. Fro brought with him Bruno's latest maps. They showed a new line of five columns, then a gap, and then two more columns. The columns were about twenty-one feet apart and could mean a huge building one hundred and fifty or more feet long. The columns on the Temple of Neptune at Paestum are about twenty-two feet apart on the ends and fifteen on the sides and the temple is two hundred feet long. At one end of our new building was a wall making a right angle. The determination that these were columns was made by drilling in a circle around them. I am sure we struck only the base of these columns as they were hit at a uniform depth in the living level.

We all flew down to Bari the next morning and stopped at the ruins of Metapontum on our way to Sybaris. These were contemporaneous with Sybaris, and many columns of a temple are still standing, along with the remains of walls of the buildings. We went direct to Giuseppe's house at Sybaris. He operated the drill while his brother, Domenico, added the four-and-one-half-foot sections as the drill went down into the soil. The men and the tractor were just coming home from work as we arrived. They were unreservedly enthusiastic about the work and how quickly they could operate and move the drill, and they had lost no time from breakdowns. It was a joy to hear after all the trouble and days of time lost in the past. We arranged for Bruno to join us at the Jolly Hotel at Castrovillari, and on the way home we stopped to see Signor Mueller. We were distressed to find that he had been seriously ill and would shortly have to return to the hospital for a further operation. Such a modest man he had never written us a word about it.

I find my diary, written that night, says, "Bruno had fantastic news for us. He had hit large areas of structures and was very sure of his columns and their location. He drilled around each one. They were all 7.6 meters apart. The length of the area covered to the corner wall was 125 meters and the width 94 meters. The width of the individual columns was two meters. The whole area of the city, outlined so far, was about four kilometers on each side and over one in width. Larger than Athens. In going over the maps with Bruno and overlaying Beth's map we found that where he was striking buildings corresponded exactly with her magnetometer findings. The problem now is that columns three hundred feet apart could not possibly be from the same building, nor could any temple be four hundred feet long. At supper we reconstructed the plan with pellets of bread for the column bases and pieces of grissini for walls. It occurred to me that what we might have were two temples a couple of hundred feet apart the way they are at Paestum, or it might be that one was a stoa and the other a temple. The walls are all run-

*Bruno, Giuseppe, Domenico, Susy, Fro,*
*and Anne with the New Drill*

ning due east and west which is just what we want. (Fro now
had a plethora of large structures for his report.)

"We decided to drill the area intensively, starting in the
spaces between the columns to try and find more columns."

The next day we went down to the dig to a day of disappointment and frustration. Bruno had marked the holes
with stakes, and measured from fixed points at the end and
side of the field. We arrived to find that the owner had
plowed the day before—they plow very deep in Italy—and
there was not a sign of a marker anywhere. Poor Bruno was
in despair, as he was naturally very proud of what he had
done and now he could not show us anything and we might
even wonder if he had really hit such a huge building. The

farmer made no objection to our continuing to work, and my diary says, "Bruno took bearings and struck a wall in the first hole. We then tried to find the line of columns from this and during the day must have drilled thirty holes without finding anything. We all went to Bagamoyo for lunch and a swim, and then back to the dig. I used my compass, based on the first hole, to a line due west. As we were about to quit, the last boring hit another wall. Home at 7:30, a long day."

At early breakfast the next morning we agreed to employ an engineer to survey the exact location of any structure we hit so that it could always be easily located. We had him at work in the morning. I arranged for Professor Foti to come from Reggio, a distance of over two hundred miles, to lunch with us the next day. I left Susy and Anne Ingersoll at Bagamoyo for a swim and went on to the dig where another morning was wasted without finding anything. After lunch Fro took the three of us on a very steep climb up one of the foothills of the Apennines at Francavilla. There we saw the remaining walls of a temple and buildings which even predated Sybaris. We picked up some interesting small bits of seventh-century B.C. sherds which were fine pottery as they were the residue of what had been thrown out of the temple and could be distinguished from the everyday commoner household pottery. From this hill we had a magnificent view of the plain. We returned to the home of Domenico and Giuseppe's parents where we were royally entertained in their living–dining room–kitchen with glasses of wine to celebrate the finding of four more columns while we were climbing the hill. Bruno felt much happier and so did we.

Everything was now moving rapidly and satisfactorily. The engineer was locating the holes and was going to place cement markers; the walls lined up in a direct east and west line. I was still trying to find columns halfway between the

known ones, and while I was working the drill it stopped at
an obstruction. My excitement was great, but I made a further try and the drill went right on through. Evidently only
one of the large and heavy roof tiles. We all met Professor
Foti and his son at Bagamoyo for lunch. He and Fro went
over the maps carefully, and Fro pointed out to him all the
places where buildings had been found by the drill and where
the magnetometer readings showed more structures. I drew
up an agreement which Anne Ingersoll translated into Italian
and which Professor Foti and Fro both signed. It called for
Professor Foti to come to Philadelphia in the winter, after
Fro had prepared his report containing all the scientific proof
of the finding of the site of Sybaris. Professor Foti would
address a meeting at the Museum announcing the discovery,
and Dr. Rainey would also speak on the work he had done.
The announcement would be given to the Italian newspapers
on the same day as it was given to the American papers, as
we did not want any possible misunderstanding with the
Italian Government that we had made any news release before they had the opportunity to do it in Italy. Professor
Foti also agreed to do everything possible to start excavating in the spring of 1969 with the financial assistance of the
"Cassa del Mezzogiorno." This is a government-sponsored
body for the development of the southern area of Italy, and
it delighted me because, if large-scale results were to be
achieved, the expense would be enormous and far beyond any
hope of private financing. If the Italian Government accomplished significant results in excavating the city which we had
found, and which had been sought unsuccessfully for so long,
it would provide a great tourist attraction and help to bring
to life this semiforgotten area of their country.

We went back to the site after lunch to find that the
drill had struck a stone structure halfway between two "col-

umns." It was very evident that it was a large building. Professor Foti sent for his archaeologist from Metapontum to discuss the spring digging, and we offered the use of our pumps and generator. Of course, Professor Foti had seen, and was thoroughly familiar with, all our problems with the water. I must admit feeling a certain sympathy with his archaeologist who, I felt, had no idea of the almost insuperable difficulties he would be faced with in the spring. However, if the Government would do it on a sufficiently large scale, perhaps building a huge dam, much might be accomplished. Removing fifteen feet of mud from what was really a subterranean lake over an area six miles in circumference was not going to be easy.

I went to bed that night with very mixed feelings. The joy of finding Sybaris after ten years of study, work, hope, and disappointment was mixed with a sense of anticlimax that we could see no great temple. On the other hand, I was glad that the further problems of excavation were now the responsibility of someone else. Finally, there was a certain sadness that the years of intense interest and emotion had now come to an end.

In another couple of days we went down to the field where the men were working, thanked them for all the successful efforts they had made, and said good-by. Would we ever be back again? Surely yes, if the Italians go ahead with the work. It will be an exciting sight when one of the great buildings begins to come to light. Some say that we will never know what lies hidden, but I have a firm belief that means will be found to uncover what treasures may lie there. Enormous strides are being made every year, and we have proved this in the past eight years. In 1961 it was unthinkable that we could detect anomalies at a depth of twenty feet, and it was equally impossible for the earlier archaeologists to have excavated the long wall.

A news article appeared later saying that Professor Foti had asked for the sum of 295,000,000 lira from the Cassa del Mezzogiorno and that at their last meeting the Cassa had approved the project. This amounts to over $400,000, and with reasonable ingenuity on the part of the engineers a way may be found to keep the water down. All sorts of plans went through my head, and it was hard for me to realize that any further suggestions on my part were not called for. Two enormous sump pits, bentonite or similar material to harden the sides, and more and larger pumps than we had used might accomplish the task. I think that it can be done and that some day Sybaris will come to light. The most I could hope for would be fallen columns of temples, which, as in other Greek temples, could be rebuilt; possibly, wonderful pieces of statuary and bronze. When one thinks of the enormous value of such articles, the prosperity brought to the area by those who would come to see the city, the expenditure of a million dollars or more would be well repaid. The Italian Government has inaugurated a vast program to bring industry to the plain of the Crati. They have already embarked on building a huge port and are making efforts to bring life to this neglected part of the country. The archaeologists may not agree with me, but I have always been an optimist and hope I will see the day when this all comes true.

When we returned to Rome, I had a talk with Dr. Donato, who discussed the possibility of our working on certain other Greek sites in Sicily. Professor Foti had further cities in Calabria and Dottoressa Zancani had sites below Paestum, all awaiting the magnetometer and the archaeologist. On discussing these sites, I realized how fortunate we had been in choosing Sybaris. There is no other lost Greek city which can compare with it in fame, size, and luxury, and about which so much was written in olden times. Not being an archaeologist, I was also interested in the history and romance of the site, and the challenge presented to find it after a hundred years of expeditions from other countries seeking it. Finally I feel sure that, if found, the richness of the city will provide many superbly beautiful objects which will give pleasure and interest to generations to come. Although I feel this way, those with more experience tell me I am wrong. I have been before! My grandchildren may learn the answer. I hope the reader will remember what I said earlier. I know nothing of archaeology, and when Dr. Rainey, Professor Foti, and other distinguished experts say that this is Sybaris, then it is Sybaris to me.

After we returned home, and before any public announcement of the discovery, Fro wrote me the following letter summarizing his conclusions:

"Following our discussions in Sybaris last month, I should like to state very simply here what I now conclude regarding the precise location of the ruins of archaic Greek Sybaris. In the conclusions of our 1960–1965 report called 'The Search for Sybaris' I wrote that the concentration of archaic pottery in the Parco del Cavallo area undoubtedly marked the site of the ancient port of Sybaris, but since we had found no remains of temples or other major public buildings such as those at Metapontum, Paestum, and so forth, we could not conclusively prove that this was the site of the city itself as well as the port.

"In three years of research since that was written, we carried out a very extensive reconnaissance of the plain with a cesium magnetometer, and most recently with a high-speed drill. Now we know that there is a concentration of archaic

Greek building foundations in the northern sector of the Parco del Cavallo area, which include the remains of major constructions, and hence I am now convinced that this is sufficient evidence for a precise location of the ancient Greek city. Let me add that the presence of archaic Greek pottery fragments all over the Parco del Cavallo area, that is, extending for about three kilometers, clearly marks the extent of the archaic city. However, we now know that all of the southern sector, that is, from the Stombi Road to south of the Crati, has been over-built in Hellenic and Roman times, so that it is impossible to detect the ruins of archaic buildings below all of that subsequent construction. Moreover, our drilling of this entire area indicates that the Raikes theory of original construction on a line of shore dunes which sank some three meters is quite certainly correct. Thus it is probable that the southern part of the original city of Sybaris was largely destroyed by the inrush of the sea over the subsiding dunes, and that only the northern sector, that is, north of the Stombi Road, was not completely inundated.

"As you know, I cannot conceive of any practical way of carrying out large-scale systematic excavations of the archaic ruins which remain north of the Stombi. Even with vastly expensive caissons embedded around a section of these ruins, the water pressure in the sands below the clay would drown any normal excavation. Hence, the only reasonable possibility is another very limited sounding in a small section of the major ruins north of the Stombi. This will be done by the Superintendent of Antiquities in the spring of 1969, but I am convinced it will in no way alter our present conclusions about the precise location of archaic Sybaris.

"So, this is it. We terminate eight years of investigation with the precise location of Sybaris, and with the development on the Sybaris plain of a highly successful instrument, a cesium magnetometer for wide-ranging underground exploration. Personally, I am very pleased with the results, and only regret that we cannot expose for you a series of those charming metopes in terracotta where dancing girls with their sly smiles could at least reassure you that all the money you have spent was worthwhile. I am sure they are there somewhere, and I hate to think of them forever buried in the mud of the Crati."

I do not like to disagree with an expert, but I cannot accept his statement that "the only reasonable possibility is another very limited sounding [excavation] in a small section." Modern engineering techinques, amply financed, should be able to solve the problem of the water. Once the method is found, what archaeological treasures may be unearthed, buried for twenty-five hundred years.

Bruno continued the drilling until the early part of November when the rain came and it was no longer possible to go into the fields. His reports were all good and contained such comments as, "I thought that next week I would have finished finding new walls, but that is not the case, as in drilling in the vicinity of the walls already found we have seen that there are many larger than we found at first. One wall, which the first time had a limit of eight meters, we now find continues for twenty-six meters [eighty-seven feet] in a very strange form." A week later he reports, "We have found other columns in the vicinity of those we already found when you were here; they are about six meters from the old ones. The more holes we make the more new constructions we come upon, always in the same zone which you know. I hope very much we can find all the construction because the zone has demonstrated that it is a very important one." Again he says, "The zone in which we are working is always the same. Around some of the walls we have also found

several hard places which later the point of the drill has passed
through; they have a very strange form which we have not
been able to understand." In the next report he told us,
"Today we have finished finding the limits of another building; it is at the same depth as all the others, and we brought
up many sherds and pieces of brick."

The map on page 195 will show that an irregular area
has been outlined which is approximately thirty-two hundred
meters long (about 1.8 miles) in the north and south direction by twenty-three hundred meters (about 1.4 miles) east
and west, with a total circumference of about 5.7 miles. (A
century later the walls of Athens were about 5.5 miles in
circumference.) Over this entire area archaic sherds were
found, a concentration of buildings in the northeast corner
was struck at the same level as these sherds, and an archaic
building of the time of Sybaris was excavated.

With all this proof at hand Professor Foti came to
America and he and Dr. Rainey announced the discovery at
a meeting of the Members of the University Museum on
December 12. The news aroused widespread interest, and
inquiries and requests for further information began coming
in from all over the world. I had letters and telephone
calls from as far west as California and received several suggestions from engineers and others as to how to cope with
the water. In a burst of enthusiasm one history professor at
a New England college wrote, "This discovery . . . must be
for this century what Troy was for the nineteenth."

With the announcement, and the commitment of the
Italians to excavate, our work had come to an end. The eight
years had provided me with intense interest and excitement,
also the possibility of learning something about archaeology
and a great deal about the ancient Greeks. Beth Ralph and
Fro Rainey had provided archaeologists with the cesium mag-

netometer, and thereby with a new method which should revolutionize the future search for ancient tombs and ruins. I am grateful for the opportunity of intimacy with Fro, an exceptional man, and for the kindness shown to me by so many others during these years. Of one thing I am sure: When we start to look for another Greek city, it will be on high land with no problem of water.

One lovely fall day I was standing watching the work. The sea and sun were at my back with the rugged mountains rising in the distance through a faint haze across the plain. This was the same beautiful scene that had brought the Greeks to this spot so many hundreds of years ago, and thoughts of the past kept recurring. These silent fields had been the setting where there had been life and activity, slavery, riches and decadence, and the site of the largest Greek city of its time. The life and culture of these people were to influence the Western World for countless ages, although here they had disappeared and, until now, had left no trace of themselves or their very existence. Domenico was removing dirt from the bit of the drill when, with his shy smile, he held out to me a tiny object. It was a small piece of charred bone. Realization came to me of what this could mean. The priest in his magnificent robes had stood on this spot, sacrificing a calf before the altar. The great door of the temple behind me was open, and the sun, as it rose from the sea, was reflected from the golden statue of the god enshrined at the western end. I had been given a token from the god by one whose ancestors lay beneath this soil. What further proof did I need?

Keats, in his "Ode on a Grecian Urn," might almost have had Sybaris in mind when he wrote:

"Who are these coming to the sacrifice?
To what green altar, O mysterious priest,
Lead'st thou that heifer lowing at the skies,
And all her silken flanks with garland drest?
What little town by river or sea shore,
Or mountain-built with peaceful citadel,
Is emptied of this folk, this pious morn?
And, little town, thy streets for evermore
Will silent be; and not a soul to tell
Why thou art desolate, can e'er return."

We had returned.

TELOS KAI ARCHE

# REFERENCE NOTES

1. Herodotus *Histories* I. 57.
2. Thucydides *History of the Peloponnesian War* I. 2.
3. Athenaeus *Deipnosophistae* IV. 138.
4. Plutarch *Parallel Lives* "Pelopidas" I. 3-4.
5. Aristotle *Politics* V. 3. 11; Strabo *Geography* VI. 1. 13; Solinus *Collectanea Rerum Memorabilium* VII.
6. Strabo *Geography* VIII. 7. 1-2; Diodorus *Universal History* XV. 48. 1-4; Ovid *Metamorphoses* XV. 293; Pliny the Elder *Natural History* II. XCIII. 206; Pausanias *Description of Greece* XXIV (Achaia). 5.
7. Herodotus *Histories* I. 146.
8. Justinus *History of Trogus Pompeius* XX. 2.
9. Scylax *Geographici Graeci Minores*, Fragment 13.
10. Herodotus *Histories* I. 145.
11. Pausanias *Description of Greece* VII (Achaia). 25. 11; Solinus *Crathis* VII.
12. Pausanias *Description of Greece* VIII (Arcadia). 15. 9.
13. Pseudo Scymnus 20. 340-41.
14. Dionysius of Halicarnassus *Roman Antiquities* XIX. 1 (17, 1).
15. Strabo *Geography* VI. 1. 12.
16. Strabo *Geography* VI. 1. 13.
17. Diodorus *Universal History* XI. 90. 3.
18. Athenaeus *Deipnosophistae* XII. 519.
19. Athenaeus *Deipnosophistae* XII. 520.
20. Athenaeus *Deipnosophistae* XII. 519.
21. Athenaeus *Deipnosophistae* XII. 519.
22. Strabo *Geography* VIII. 7. 4.
23. Ovid *Fasti* III. 581; Ovid *Metamorphoses* XIV. 315; Pseudo

Scymnus 339; Strabo Geography VIII. 7. 4, 5; Pliny the Elder Natural History XXXI. 10. 14; Dionysius of Halicarnassus Roman Antiquities XIX. 1. (17. 1); Pausanias Description of Greece VII (Achaia). 25. 11; Diodorus Universal History XI. 90. 3; Herodotus Histories I. 145; Scylax Geographici Graeci Minores, Fragment 13; Aristotle De Mirabilibus Auscultationibus 169; Ovid Fasti III. 581; Strabo Geography VI. 1. 13.

24. Ovid Fasti III. 581.
25. Aristotle De Mirabilibus Auscultationibus 169.
26. Pliny the Elder Natural History XXXI. 9. 13; Aelian On the Nature of Animals XII. 36.
27. Pliny the Elder Natural History XXXI. 10. 14.
28. Athenaeus Deipnosophistae VI. 269.
29. Diodorus Universal History XII. 9.
30. Pliny the Elder Natural History XVIII. 65.
31. Varro De Re Rustica I. 44. 2.
32. Athenaeus Deipnosophistae XIV. 656.
33. Strabo Geography VI. 1. 14; Pliny the Elder Natural History XIV. 8. 69.
34. Athenaeus Deipnosophistae I. 34.
35. Pliny the Elder Natural History XIV. 4. 39.
36. Herodotus Histories V. 45.
37. Strabo Geography V. 4. 13.
38. Athenaeus Deipnosophistae XII. 520.
39. Strabo Geography VI. 1. 13; Diodorus Universal History XII. 9.
40. Aristotle Politics V. 3. 11.
41. Justinus History of Trogus Pompeius XX. 2.
42. Diodorus Universal History XII. 9.
43. Pseudo Scymnus 339.
44. Diodorus Universal History XII. 9.
45. Strabo Geography VI. 1. 13.
46. Athenaeus Deipnosophistae XII. 525.
47. Athenaeus Deipnosophistae XII. 523.
48. Athenaeus Deipnosophistae XII. 522.
49. Athenaeus Deipnosophistae IV. 128.
50. Hesiod Shield of Heracles 272.

51. Euripides *Helen* 722.
52. Athenaeus *Deipnosophistae* IV. 128.
53. Aelian *On the Nature of Animals* XVI. 23.
54. Athenaeus *Deipnosophistae* XII. 518.
55. Athenaeus *Deipnosophistae* XII. 519.
56. Athenaeus *Deipnosophistae* XII. 521.
57. Diodorus *Universal History* VIII. 18. 2.
58. Diodorus *Universal History* VIII. 18. 2.
59. Athenaeus *Deipnosophistae* XII. 521.
60. Athenaeus *Deipnosophistae* XII. 521.
61. Lucian *The Ignorant Book Collector* 23.
62. Athenaeus *Deipnosophistae* XII. 519.
63. Athenaeus *Deipnosophistae* XII. 519.
64. Athenaeus *Deipnosophistae* XII. 519.
65. Athenaeus *Deipnosophistae* XII. 519.
66. Athenaeus *Deipnosophistae* XII. 518.
67. Athenaeus *Deipnosophistae* XII. 520.
68. Athenaeus *Deipnosophistae* VI. 273.
69. Aelian *Varia Historia* XII. 24; Athenaeus *Deipnosophistae* XII. 541; Herodotus *Histories* VI. 127.
70. Diodorus *Universal History* VIII. 19.
71. Athenaeus *Deipnosophistae* XII. 523 (quoting Homer).
72. Herodotus *Histories* VI. 21.
73. Athenaeus *Deipnosophistae* XII. 541 (quoting Aristotle *Wonders* 96).
74. Athenaeus *Deipnosophistae* XII. 518.
75. Athenaeus *Deipnosophistae* XII. 519.
76. Athenaeus *Deipnosophistae* XII. 521.
77. Athenaeus *Deipnosophistae* XII. 519.
78. Athenaeus *Deipnosophistae* XII. 519.
79. Aelian *On the Nature of Animals* VI. 10. XVI. 23; Athenaeus *Deipnosophistae* XII. 520.
80. Diodorus *Universal History* VIII. 18; Athenaeus *Deipnosophistae* XII. 518.
81. Athenaeus *Deipnosophistae* XII. 518.
82. Seneca the Younger *On Anger* II. 25. 2.
83. Seneca the Younger *On Anger* II. 25. 2.
84. Diodorus *Universal History* VIII. 20.

85. Strabo Geography V. 4. 13.
86. Virgil Georgics IV. 119.
87. Pliny the Elder Natural History XV. 1.
88. Diodorus Universal History V. 40. 3.
89. Athenaeus Deipnosophistae XII. 517.
90. Diodorus Universal History V. 13. 1–2.
91. Virgil Aeneid X. 174; Strabo Geography V. 2. 6.
92. Virgil Aeneid VIII. 483.
93. Strabo Geography VI. 1. 1
94. Sophocles Antigone 737.
95. Athenaeus Deipnosophistae XII. 520.
96. Stephanus Byzantinus Ethnica Sub. V. 134; Athenaeus Deipnosophistae XII. 520.
97. Pseudo Scymnus 339.
98. Athenaeus Deipnosophistae XII. 522.
99. Pseudo Scymnus 339.
100. Pausanias Description of Greece V (Elis I). 8, 9.
101. Strabo Geography VIII. 7. 5.
102. Strabo Geography VI. 1. 12; Diodorus Universal History VIII. 17. 2.
103. Diodorus Universal History XII. 9. 2.
104. Diodorus Universal History XII. 9. 2.
105. Athenaeus Deipnosophistae XII. 521.
106. Athenaeus Deipnosophistae XII. 521.
107. Athenaeus Deipnosophistae XII. 521.
108. Heraclides Ponticus Fragmenta Historicorum Graecorum 199, Fragment V. 2; Athenaeus Deipnosophistae XII. 521.
109. Diodorus Universal History XII. 9. 2; Strabo Geography VI. 1. 13.
110. Aelian On the Nature of Animals XVI. 23; Athenaeus Deipnosophistae XII. 520; Aristotle Fragments 583 (Rose).
111. Diodorus Universal History XII. 10.
112. Strabo Geography VI. 1. 13 .
113. Diodorus Universal History XI. 48. 4.
114. Herodotus Histories V. 44.
115. Herodotus Histories V. 45; Eratosthenes Fragmenta Chronologica.
116. Stephanus Byzantinus Ethnica s.v. Thurii.

117. Diodorus *Universal History* XII. 10. XI. 90. 3–4; Strabo *Geography* VI. 1. 13.
118. Diodorus *Universal History* XII. 10. 3.
119. Diodorus *Universal History* XII. 10. 5.
120. Diodorus *Universal History* XII. 10. 6.
121. Diodorus *Universal History* XII. 10. 7.
122. Strabo *Geography* VI. 1. 13; Diodorus *Universal History* XII. 10. 7.
123. Diodorus *Universal History* XII. 11.
124. Diodorus *Universal History* XII. 11.
125. Diodorus *Universal History* XII. 35.
126. Justinus *History of Trogus Pompeius* XX. 1.
127. Philostratus *In Honor of Apollonius of Tyana* III. 15.
128. Diodorus *Universal History* XII. 11.
129. Diodorus *Universal History* XII. 12.
130. Plutarch *Moralia: On Curiosity* 519, 8c; Diodorus *Universal History* XII. 11, 12.
131. Aristotle *Politics* V. 6. 6.
132. Aristotle *Politics* V. 7. 12.
133. Xenophon *Hellenica* I. 5. 19.
134. Appian *Hannibalic War* VI. 34.
135. Athenaeus *Deipnosophistae* XI. 474.
136. Cicero *Ad Atticum* IX. 2. III. 5.
137. Thucydides *History of the Peloponnesian War* VII. 33. 5.
138. Thucydides *History of the Peloponnesian War* VIII. 35. 1.
139. Thucydides *History of the Peloponnesian War*. VIII. 61. 2.
140. Thucydides *History of the Peloponnesian War* VIII. 84. 2.
141. Thucydides *History of the Peloponnesian War* VI. 61. 6.
142. Plutarch *Parallel Lives* "Alcibiades" XXII. 1.
143. Diodorus *Universal History* XIV. 101. 1.
144. Diodorus *Universal History* XVI. 15. 2.
145. Livy *Histories* X. 2.
146. Pliny the Elder *Natural History* XXXIV. 15. 32.
147. Appian *Samnite History* VII. 1.
148. Appian *Hannibalic War* I. 4.
149. Livy *Histories* XXI. 38. 2.
150. Appian *Hannibalic War* IV. 25.
151. Appian *Hannibalic War* VI. 32.

152. Appian *Hannibalic War* VI. 34.
153. Appian *Hannibalic War* VIII. 49.
154. Appian *Hannibalic War* VIII. 52.
155. Appian *Hannibalic War* IX. 57.
156. Appian *Hannibalic War* IX. 59.
157. Livy *Histories* XXVIII. 15. 12.
158. Polybius *Histories* XI. 19.
159. Appian *Civil Wars* I. 14. 116–20; Livy *Histories* Sum. XCV. 96. 97.
160. Procopius *Bellum Gothicum* VII. 28. 8.
161. Livy *Histories* XXV. 15. 7–17.
162. Athenaeus *Deipnosophistae* XII. 520.
163. Athenaeus *Deipnosophistae* XII. 519.

# BIBLIOGRAPHY

ALETTI, EZIO, Sibari. Rome: A. Garzanti, 1960–62.

ASIMOV, ISAAC, The Greeks: A Great Adventure. Boston: Houghton Mifflin Company, 1965.

BARR, STRINGFELLOW, The Will of Zeus. Philadelphia: J. B. Lippincott Company, 1961.

BÉRARD, JEAN, L'Expansion et la Colonisation Grècques. Paris: Aubier, 1960.

BOARDMAN, JOHN, The Greeks Overseas. Baltimore: Penguin Books, Inc., 1964.

BOWRA, C. M., Classical Greece. New York: Time-Life Books, 1965.

——, The Greek Experience. New York: The New American Library, 1957.

CALLAWAY, JOSEPH S., Sybaris. Baltimore: Johns Hopkins Press, 1950.

CANDIDO, MARIO, Valle Crati. Venice, Italy: Scuola Grafica, Instituto Salesiano, 1967.

CERAM, C. W., Gods, Graves, and Scholars. New York: Alfred A. Knopf, 1951.

——, The March of Archaeology. Translated from the German by Richard and Clara Winston. New York: Alfred A. Knopf, 1958.

—— (ed.), Hands on the Past. New York: Alfred A. Knopf, 1966.

CIACERI, EMANUELE, Storia Della Magna Grecia. Milan: Albrighi Segati and Company.

DUNBABIN, T. J., The Western Greeks. Oxford: The Clarendon Press, 1948.

DURANT, WILL, *The Life of Greece*. New York: Simon & Schuster, 1939.

EVANS, ARTHUR JOHN, *The Palace of Minos*. London: Macmillan, 1921–35.

GIANNELLI, GIULIO, *Culti e Miti della Magna Grecia*. Florence: Sansoni, 1963.

GIBBON, EDWARD, *The History of the Decline and Fall of the Roman Empire*.

HALE, EDWARD EVERETT, *Sybaris and Other Homes*. Boston: Fields, Osgood and Company, 1869.

HALE, WILLIAM HARLAN, *The Horizon Book of Ancient Greece*. New York: American Heritage Publishing Company, Inc., 1965.

HAMILTON, EDITH, *The Greek Way*. New York: W. W. Norton & Company, Inc., 1930.

HARREL-COURTES, HENRY, *Etruscan Italy*. Translated by James Hogarth. New York: Orion Press, 1964.

HAWKES, JACQUETTA (ed.), *The World of the Past*. Translated from the French by James Hogarth. New York: Alfred A. Knopf, 1963.

HEURGON, JACQUES, *Daily Life of the Etruscans*. Translated from the French by James Kirkup. New York: The Macmillan Company, 1964.

HOCKE, GUSTAV RENÉ, *Sybaris*. Munich: Nymphenburger Verlaggs Handlung, 1949.

JOHNSTONE, M. A., *Etruria Past and Present*. London: Methuen & Company, Ltd., 1930.

KITTO, H. D. F., *The Greeks*. Baltimore: Penguin Books, Inc., 1951.

LAMB, HAROLD, *Hannibal: One Man Against Rome*. New York: Doubleday Company, 1958.

LENORMANT, FRANÇOIS, *La Grande Grèce*. Paris: A. Levy, 1881.

LISSNER, IVAR, *The Living Past*. Translated from the German by J. Maxwell Brownjohn. New York: G. P. Putnam, 1957.

MACKENDRICK, PAUL L., *The Greek Stones Speak*. New York: St. Martins Press, Inc., 1962.

MONTUORO, PAOLA ZANCANI, and M. W. STOOP, *Scavi a Francavilla Marittima*. Rome: Societa Magna Grecia, 1966.

PAYNE, ROBERT, *The Gold of Troy*: The Story of Heinrich Schliemann and the Buried Cities of Ancient Greece. New York: Funk and Wagnalls Co., 1958.

——, *Lost Treasures of the Mediterranean World*. New York: Thomas Nelson & Sons, 1962.

PERRET, JACQUES, *Siris*. Paris: Société d'Edition "Les Belles Lettres," 1941.

RAINEY, FROELICH G., CARLO M. LERICI, and ORVILLE H. BULLITT. *The Search for Sybaris*. Rome: Lerici Editori, 1967.

RANDALL-MACIVER, DAVID, *Greek Cities in Italy and Sicily*. Oxford: The Clarendon Press, 1931.

ROBSJOHN-GIBBINGS, TERENCE H., and CARLTON W. PULLIN, *Furniture of Classical Greece*. New York: Alfred A. Knopf, 1964.

ST. JOHN, JAMES A., *The History of the Manners and Customs of Ancient Greece*, 1842.

SCHREIBER, HERMANN and GEORGE, *Vanished Cities*. Translated from the German by Richard and Clara Winston. New York: Alfred A. Knopf, 1957.

SESTIERI, PELLEGRINO CLAUDIO, *Paestum*. Rome: Libreria Dello Stat.

STOBART, J. C., *The Glory That Was Greece*. Philadelphia: J. B. Lippincott Co., 1911.

TAYLOUR, WILLIAM O., *The Mycenaeans*. London: Thames and Hudson, Ltd., 1964.

TUCKER, THOMAS G., *Life in Ancient Athens*. New York: Macmillan, 1906.

WOODHEAD, A. G., *The Greeks in the West*. New York: Frederick A. Praeger, Inc., 1962.

ZIMMERN, ALFRED E., *The Greek Commonwealth*. Oxford: Clarendon Press, 1915.

ZSCHIETZSCHMANN, WILLY, *Hellas and Rome*. New York: Universe Books, 1960.

In addition to the above, there are numerous articles and pamphlets in various languages on the subject of Sybaris.

Recent Techical Publications on Magnetometers
and Thermoluminescence

Aitken, M. J., *Physics and Archaeology*. Interscience Publishers, New York, 1961.

Breiner, Sheldon, "The Rubidium Magnetometer in Archaeological Exploration," *Science*, October 8, 1965.

Rainey, Froelich G., and Elizabeth K. Ralph, "Archaeology and Its New Technology," *Science*, September 23, 1966.

Ralph, Elizabeth K., "Comparison of a Proton and a Rubidium Magnetometer for Archaeological Prospecting," *Archaeometry*, vol. 7, 1965, Bulletin of the Research Laboratory for Archaeology and the History of Art, Oxford University.

——, "The Electronic Detective and the Case of the Missing City," *Expedition*, University Museum, Philadelphia, Winter, 1965

——, and Mark C. Han, "Dating of Pottery by Thermoluminescence," *Nature*, London, April 16, 1966.

—— and ——, "Potential of Thermoluminescence Dating." Paper read at annual meeting of the American Chemical Society, Atlantic City, N.J., 1968.

——, Frank Morrison, and Douglas P. O'Brien, "Archaeological Surveying Utilizing a High-Sensitivity Difference Magnetometer," *Geoexploration*, Elsevier Publishing Co., Amsterdam 1968.

# ANCIENT AUTHORS

AELIAN
Late IIc.–Early IIIc. A.D.
AMMIANUS MARCELLINUS
ca. A.D. 325–ca. 392
ANDOCIDES
ca. 440–ca. 390 B.C.
ANTIOCHUS
ca. Vc. B.C.
APOLLODORUS
ca. 140 B.C.
APPIAN
ca. A.D. 100
ARISTOPHANES
ca. 448–385 B.C.
ARISTOTLE
384–322 B.C.
ATHENAEUS
Late IIc.–Early IIIc. A.D.
CAESAR
100–44 B.C.
CICERO
106–43 B.C.
CLEMENT OF ALEXANDRIA
Late IIc.–Early IIIc. A.D.
DEMOSTHENES
ca. 384–322 B.C.
DIO CASSIUS
Late IIc.–Early IIIc. A.D.

DIO CHRYSOSTOM
ca. A.D. 40–ca. 115
DIODORUS SICULUS
ca. 80–20 B.C.
DIONYSIUS OF HALICARNASSUS
ca. 54–7 B.C.
EPHORUS
400–330 B.C.
ERATOSTHENES
ca. 276–ca. 194 B.C.
EURIPIDES
480–406 B.C.
EUSEBIUS
ca. A.D. 260–ca. 340
FLORUS
ca. A.D. 100
HERACLIDES PONTICUS
ca. IVc. B.C.
HERODOTUS
ca. 484–425 B.C.
HESIOD
ca. VIIIc. B.C.
HOMER

IAMBLICHUS
ca. IVc. A.D.
ISIDORUS OF SEVILLE
ca. A.D. 570–636

JORDANES
  ca. VIc. A.D.
JUSTINUS
  ca. A.D. 100
JUVENAL
  ca. A.D. 60–140
LIVY
  59 B.C.–A.D. 17
LUCIAN
  ca. A.D. 120–ca. 180
LYCOPHRON
  285–247 B.C.
MAXIMUS OF TYRE
  ca. IIc. A.D.
MELA
  ca. Ic. A.D.
MENANDER
  ca. 343–ca. 292 B.C.
NEPOS
  99–24 B.C.
OVID
  43 B.C.–A.D. 17
PAUSANIAS
  ca. IIc. A.D.
PHILO OF ALEXANDRIA
  ca. 20 B.C.
PHILOSTRATUS
  ca. A.D. 170–ca. 245
PHOTIUS
  ca. IXc. A.D.
PINDAR
  ca. 522–ca. 443 B.C.
PLATO
  428/27–348/47 B.C.
PLINY THE ELDER
  ca. A.D. 23–79
PLUTARCH
  ca. A.D. 46–ca. 120

POLYAENUS
  ca. IIc. A.D.
POLYBIUS
  ca. 204–ca. 122 B.C.
PROCOPIUS
  ca. VIc. A.D.
PSEUDO SCYMNUS
  ca. 90 B.C.
PTOLEMAEUS
  ca. A.D. 125
PYTHAGORAS
  ca. 582–ca. 500 B.C.
QUINTILIAN
  ca. A.D. 35–ca. 100
SALLUST
  86–34 B.C.
SCYLAX
  521–485 B.C.
SCYMNUS
  ca. Late IIIc.–Early IIc. B.C.
SENECA THE YOUNGER
  ca. 4 B.C.–ca. A.D. 65
SOLINUS
  ca. IIIc. A.D.
SOPHOCLES
  495–406 B.C.
STEPHANUS BYZANTINUS
  Early VIc. A.D.
STRABO
  64/63 B.C.–After A.D. 21
SUETONIUS
  ca. A.D. 100
SUIDAS
  ca. Xc. A.D.
TACITUS
  ca. A.D. 55–ca. 120

TERTULLIAN
    ca. A.D. 155–ca. 222
THEOCRITUS
    ca. IIIc. B.C.
THEON
    ca. Ic. A.D.
THEOPOMPUS OF CHIOS
    ca. 380 B.C.
THUCYDIDES
    ca. 472–ca. 399 B.C.
TIMAEUS
    ca. 345–ca. 250 B.C.
TROGUS
    ca. Ic. B.C.

VALERIUS MAXIMUS
    ca. Ic. A.D.
VARRO
    116–27 B.C.
VELLEIUS PATERCULUS
    ca. 19 B.C.–ca. A.D. 31
VIBIUS SEQUESTER
    ca. Vc. A.D.
VIRGIL
    70–19 B.C.
VITRUVIUS
    Early Ic. A.D.
XENOPHON
    ca. 434–ca. 355 B.C.

# INDEX

Achaea, 22, 24, 41, 87
Achaeans, 22, 38, 40, 79
  expel Troezenians, 45
  found Croton, 25
  found Sybaris, 24, 44
Adamasteanu, Signor, 190
Adriatic coast, 97
Adriatic Sea, 128
Aegae, 38
Aegean Islands, 22
Aegean Sea, 14, 68
Aerial photographs, of Sybaris
  plain, 10, 152, 158, 160,
  161, 170, 185, 187–88,
  190, 191, 192–93, 196,
  197, 203
  made by Italian Air Force,
  198–200
Agora, 47
Agrigentum, 70, 201
Alaric, xiv, 83
  life of, 5–6
  quest for tomb, 7–11, 32

Alcibiades, 19, 153
  life of, 123–26
Alps, 129, 154
  crossed by Hannibal, 127–28
Apennines, 25, 26, 33, 44, 72,
  98, 154, 206
Apollinara, 86, 96, 151
Aqueduct, from Fonte del Fico
  to Parco del Cavallo, 87,
  149–50, 169, 187
Archaic sherds, 86, 116, 145,
  151, 152, 161, 162, 163,
  170, 173, 177, 186, 187,
  190, 193, 194, 199, 200,
  210
Archaic structures, 174, 178,
  182, 211
Archaic zone, 201
Argentanum, silver mines at, 88
Argolis, 24
Asia Minor, 19, 20, 21, 22, 23,
  42, 49, 52, 63, 67, 75, 88

Hercules, arrows of, 112, 120, 170

Herodotus, dies at Thurii, 84

Hiero I, 72

Hieron, made general by Sybarites, 83

Hippodamus, plans Thurii, 118

Hitler, 127

Iapygia, 22

Ingersoll, Anne C., 203, 206, 207

Ionian Sea, 12, 25, 26, 44, 49, 79, 99, 123, 175

Ionians, 12, 18, 27, 60, 121
characteristics of, 19

Is of Helice (founder of Sybaris), 25

Ischia, 20, 170

Italian Government, 100, 132, 134, 143, 146, 149, 160, 161, 170, 207
claims ownership of objects found, 11, 107
contemplates drainage of Sybaris site, 159, 202, 208
makes air photographs of plain, 197–99
permission of needed for archaeological excavations, 11
requires yearly permit, 145
trouble with over press release, 164–65

Italians, 28, 34, 100, 129, 130, 132, 134, 135, 140, 144–45, 163, 164, 189, 197, 208, 213

Italic tombs, 93

Italy, xii, 6, 8, 9, 11, 12, 20, 21, 22, 25, 26, 29, 30, 38, 42, 45, 66, 68, 72, 75, 80, 97, 99, 110, 128, 154, 159, 164, 174, 177, 192, 198, 203, 205, 207

Itek Corporation (developers of camera for aerial photography), 161

Jordanes, 7, 83

Kahrstedt, Ulrich, theory of on location of Sybaris, 95, 96

Keats, John, 214–15

Kitchener, Lord, desecrates Mahdi tomb, 5

Knossos, 15
description of palace, 14
destruction of, 14
Evans excavation of, 17

Kohler, Dr. Ellen, 136, 143

Lacedaemonia, 126

Lacedaemonians, refuse to aid in founding Thurii, 117

Lao River, 76

Lattughella, 157, 160, 181

Laus (trading port colony of Sybaris), 26, 50, 68, 75–76
attacked by Lucanians, 126

Le Muraglie, 90, 96, 187

Lenormant, François, expedition of to Sybaris, 87–93, 96, 149, 150, 151

Lerici, Carlo M., 29, 101
holds press conference, 142
locates Etruscan tombs, 6, 8, 9, 99, 109
locates wall at Sybaris, 9, 10, 28
works at Sybaris site, 99–100, 102, 110, 132, 134, 145

Lerici Foundation, 109, 114, 132, 136, 149, 164

Tarentum (Taranto)
  besieged by Hannibal, 71
  defeats Thurii, 127
  falls to Hannibal, 128
  founded, 25
  lost by Hannibal, 129
Taranto, Gulf of, 25, 97
Tarquinia, Etruscan tombs excavated at, 100
Telys
  murders envoys, 81
  overthrows Sybaris rulers, 80
Themistocles, 45
Theodosius, court of, 5
Thermoluminescence technique for dating pottery, 30
Thuria spring, 118
Thurians, 119, 122, 123, 125, 126, 127
  description of, 120
Thurii, 83, 87, 90, 150, 151, 152, 153, 154, 155, 157, 160, 165, 166
  fleet of, 23
  history of, 117–30
  port of found, 186
  possible site of, 158
  ruins found by Lenormant, 89
  successor to Sybaris, 37
Thurio, 152
Thurium, 130
  founded, 118
Tiryns, 15, 16, 17
Torre Della Chiesa, 196
Torre del Mordillo, 93, 94, 104, 152, 153, 157, 175, 187
Torrenti (spring floods), 142, 144, 189
Trebisacce, 34, 199
Troezenians
  expelled from Sybaris, 45

settle Sybaris, 23, 24, 44
Trojan horse, 34
Trojan War, 124
Troy, xi, 4, 15, 16, 17, 34, 120
Turdetani, 127
Tuscany, 28, 109
Tyrrhenia, 74
Tyrrhenians, 60, 72–73
Tyrrhenian Sea, 26, 29, 31, 68, 72

U-2, 160
University of Pennsylvania Museum, 6, 8, 9, 29, 30, 31, 66, 85, 89, 93, 94, 97, 104, 108, 110, 116, 132–34, 135, 136, 138, 140, 149, 150, 160, 164, 165, 170, 180, 188, 192, 198, 199, 203

Varian Associates, 108, 174, 186, 196
  develop cesium magnetometer, 169, 174
  develop rubidium magnetometer, 110, 161
Velia (home of Eleatic philosophers), 29
Ventris, Michael, deciphers Linear B script, 17–18
Vesuvius, 29, 92, 154, 175
Viola, Luigi, drills plain (1887–88), 93

Well-point drainage, 169, 170, 178, 181, 182–83, 185

Zancle, 20. See also Messina
Zanotti-Bianco, Senator Umberto, 95, 96, 151

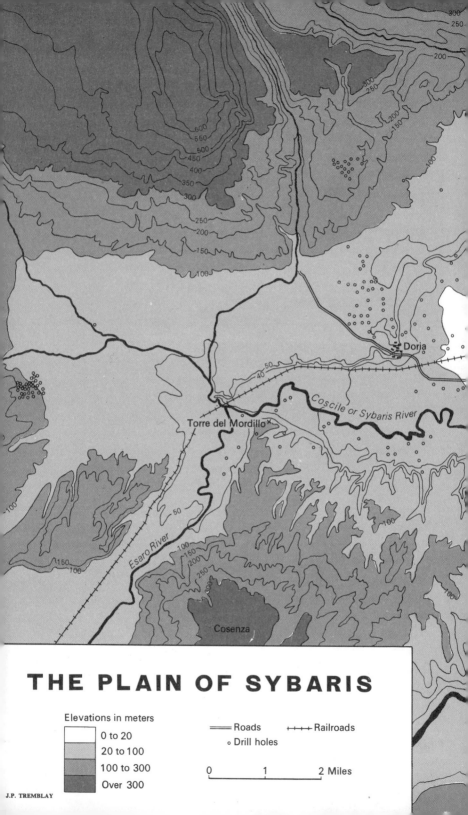

# THE PLAIN OF SYBARIS

Elevations in meters

| | |
|---|---|
| | 0 to 20 |
| | 20 to 100 |
| | 100 to 300 |
| | Over 300 |

Roads ━━━ Railroads +++++

o Drill holes

0      1      2 Miles

Dorja

Coscile or Sybaris River

Torre del Mordillo×

Esaro River

Cosenza

J.P. TREMBLAY